YOUTH EMPLOYMENT IN AMERICAN INDUSTRY

YOUTH EMPLOYMENT IN AMERICAN INDUSTRY

Robert B. Hill *and* **Regina Nixon**

Transaction Books
New Brunswick (U.S.A.) and London (U.K.)

Copyright © 1984 by the National Urban League, Inc., Research
Department, Washington, D.C. 20004.

All rights reserved under International and Pan-American Copyright
Conventions. No part of this book may be reproduced or transmitted in
any form or by any means, electronic or mechanical, including photo-
copy, recording, or any information storage and retrieval system,
without prior permission in writing from the publisher. All inquiries
should be addressed to Transaction Books, Rutgers—The State University, New Brunswick, New Jersey 08903.

Library of Congress Catalog Number: 84-2750
ISBN: 0-87855-986-8 (paper)
Printed in the United States of America

Library of Congress Cataloging in Publication Data

Hill, Robert Bernard, 1938-
  Youth employment in American industry.

  Bibliography: p.   85-7884
  1. Youth—Employment—United States. 2. Minority
youth—Employment—United States. I. Nixon, Regina.
II. Title.
HD6273.H54   1984   331.3'4'0973   84-2750
ISBN 0-87855-986-8 (pbk.)

Contents

List of Tables

Appendix D Tables

List of Figures

Foreword

Library shelves are full of dusty volumes that chronicle the gross employment problems facing young people. Minority youth, in particular, suffer from unemployment of disastrous proportions. Much of the previous research on the labor market experiences of the young in private industry, however, has been restricted to case studies or to a limited number of business establishments in a few selected locations.

The employer survey presented in this volume succeeds in filling a vacuum because it makes unique contributions to our knowledge about teenage and young adult workers in American industry. The survey yields, for the first time, nationwide and comprehensive information about corporate attitudes and practices toward youth, detailed by industry type, size, locale, and region.

We are particularly pleased to publish this volume at a time when the debate over the efficacy of a subminimum wage for youth still rages and when black youth unemployment still ranges between 40 and 50 percent. The findings of this study are directly relevant to that debate and, it is hoped, will have some influence on its outcome. The results of this and other studies show clearly that the problem of youth unemployment is far more complex than most of us have thought and the solution to that problem does not lie in the field of economics alone.

The present study was originally funded by the U.S. Department of Labor. When those funds were expended, subsequent work was underwritten entirely by the National Urban League Research Department. The work was continued despite the lack of outside funding, because we felt that the issues being addressed were important and that the data collected would suggest some short- and long-term national policy recommendations.

As current director of research at the Urban League, I am proud because this volume represents a continuing collaboration of a former director of research, Dr. Robert Hill, with the National Urban League Research Department. Hill served as principal investigator for the project that began while he was still with the Urban League; he is currently senior research associate at the Bureau of Social Science Research, Inc. Dr. Regina Nixon, a senior associate of the Research Department, served as project director and, somehow, remained calm and completed her work despite being distracted by competing demands for her time.

Finally, some words of caution. Let us take care not to let the light of this important work be consumed by the darkened cloisters of our local libraries. It is meant to be widely read and used.

James D. McGhee, director
National Urban League Research Department

Acknowledgments

We are grateful to many individuals for their assistance in bringing this project to fruition. A special thanks is due Carol Godley, research associate on the project, for her help in the design and implementation of the survey. We also appreciate Grover McDonald and Dorcas Dessaso, special assistants for the project.

We are grateful to Mildred Love and members of the Career Training and Economic Resources Department at the National Urban League for their input in the development and design of the survey. Our gratitude also extends to members of National Urban League's Commerce and Industry Council who participated in planning the study. To Michael Rosow, at the Work in America Institute, we extend our thanks for his constructive comments on the survey instrument.

We are also indebted to John Cardwell, President of EVAXX, Inc., with whom we contracted for the computer tabulations. We thank Debra Lindsay, who conducted a literature review on the youth employment problem, and Ronald Jones, who is responsible for the graphic displays. We are also grateful to Douglas Glasgow and William Haskins at the National Urban League for their critical review of the manuscript.

We extend hearty thanks to Joan Dupigny and Diane Anderson, who typed several drafts of this study.

To Diane Edwards, our Labor Department project officer, we extend our appreciation for her support and unfailing cooperation. We are especially indebted to the International Business Machines (IBM) Corporation, which provided the funds to publish this volume. Last but not least, we are indebted to Robert Taggart, former head of the Labor Department's Office of Youth Programs, for his sensitivity to the need for such a survey.

1
Highlights of Major Findings

Industrial Representation of Youths:

- Teenagers, 16-19 years old, and young adults, 20-24 years old, are concentrated in the same industries. Both groups of young workers are most concentrated in trade, service, and finance businesses and least concentrated in manufacturing and "other" (i.e., agriculture, mining, construction, and transportation) establishments.
- The proportion of young workers hired in private industry does not vary by size of business. Teenagers comprise 10% or more of all employees in about two-fifths of small (40%), medium-sized (35%), or large (37%) businesses. Similarly, young adults account for 25% or more of all employees in about two-fifths of small (41%), medium-sized (37%), or large (44%) businesses.

Occupational Representation of Youths:

- Teenagers are concentrated in clerical, service, and laborer jobs, while young adults are concentrated in clerical, service, and professional/technical/managerial occupations. Three-fourths (75%) of all businesses surveyed indicated that teenagers are most concentrated in clerical (25%), service (28%), and laborer (27%) positions. On the other hand, about two-thirds (64%) of all businesses indicated that young adults are most concentrated in clerical (23%), service (21%), and professional/technical/managerial (20%) occupations.

Hiring Guidelines for Young Workers:

- Private businesses use hiring guidelines that vary for teenagers and young adults.
- Young adults are more likely than teenagers to be hired for entry-level jobs and positions that require some experience. Eight out of 10 businesses hire young adults for entry-level positions, while only six out of 10 hire teenagers for such jobs. Only four out of 10 businesses hire teenagers for occupations requiring experience, while eight out of 10 firms hire young adults for such posts.
- However, teenagers are more likely than young adults to be hired for part-time jobs. Three-fourths of all businesses hire teens for part-time work, while only 60% hire young adults.

1

Advancement Opportunities for Young Workers:

- Young workers have the most opportunities for advancement in trade and finance industries and the least opportunities in service firms. Eight out of 10 trade (81%) and finance (85%) businesses surveyed reported that they provide "some" or "a great extent" of advancement opportunities for teenagers, compared to only six out of 10 service (60%) and "other" (59%) establishments. Similarly, almost all of the trade (96%) and finance (99%) businesses have advancement opportunities for young adults, compared to only two-thirds (68%) of service firms.
- Teenagers tend to have greater advancement opportunities in small rather than medium-sized or large businesses, while young adults tend to have more opportunities in small and large establishments than in medium-sized firms.

Occupational Representation of Minority Youths

- Two-thirds of all businesses surveyed indicated that minority youth are most concentrated in three occupations—service (28%), clerical (20%), and laborers (19%).
- Three-fourths or more of the businesses in manufacturing (90%), service (74%), and "other" (87%) industries said that minority youth held blue-collar jobs, compared to only half (51%) of the trade and one-tenth (11%) of the finance firms.

Hiring Patterns of Minority Youths

- Eight out of 10 businesses surveyed reported hiring about the same (65%) or more (14%) black youths than they did the previous year, while only two out of 10 (18%) hired fewer black youths.
- Six out of 10 businesses surveyed hired about the same (50%) or more (13%) Hispanic youths than they did the previous year, while about four out of 10 (36%) hired fewer Hispanic youths.
- Trade, finance, and service firms hire black and Hispanic youths to a greater extent than manufacturing and "other" businesses. But hiring patterns do not vary by size of business. Minority youth are more likely to be hired by firms in central cities and suburbs than by those in rural/exurban areas.
- Black youths are more likely to be hired by southern firms than by those outside the South, while Hispanic youths are more likely to be hired by western firms than by those outside the West.
- Less than 1% of the businesses surveyed currently have special jobs programs for minority youth.

Knowledge and Use of Government Jobs Programs:

- The government jobs programs that most businesses have heard of are: CETA On-the-Job Training (87%), Work Incentive (WIN) Tax

Credits (79%), Targeted Jobs Tax Credits (73%), and CETA Youth Employment and Training (66%). However, employers are least familiar with the Subminimum Wage Youth Certificates (37%) and the SPEDY Summer Youth Program (22%) for disadvantaged youths.
* The three government jobs programs that were used most frequently by private businesses are: the Targeted Jobs Tax Credits (34%), WIN Tax Credits (22%), and CETA-OJT (24%). On the other hand, less than 5% of the businesses surveyed had participated in the SPEDY Summer Youth Program (4%) or the Subminimum Wage Youth Certificate Program (3%).

Use of Targeted Jobs Tax Credits (TJTC):

* Trade businesses use the TJTC most frequently, while service firms use them least frequently. Six out of 10 (63%) trade firms use the TJTC, compared to four out of 10 manufacturing (39%) and finance (39%) firms and one out of four service (23%) and "other" (24%) businesses.
* Targeted Jobs Tax Credits are used more frequently by businesses that are small (with 50-99 employees) than by firms with 100 or more employees; by firms in suburban areas than by those in central cities or rural/exurban areas; and by firms with high proportions of young people 16-24 years old as employees.

Use of Work Incentive (WIN) Tax Credits:

* Use of WIN Tax Credits in the private sector varies little by industry. Service (31%) and manufacturing (27%) firms are about as likely as trade (25%) and finance (25%) firms to use WIN credits.
* Utilization of WIN tax credits also varies little by size or location of business. Large businesses (31%) are about as likely as medium-sized (23%) and small (25%) firms to use WIN credits. And, central city (25%) firms are just as likely as suburban (26%) and rural/exurban (24%) firms to use WIN credits.

Use of CETA On-the-Job (OJT) Training:

* CETA-OJT program was used most frequently by service firms. Four out of 10 (42%) service businesses participated in the CETA-OJT program, compared to only two out of 10 manufacturing (24%), trade (21%), and finance (22%) firms and only one out of 10 (11%) "other" businesses.
* One-third (34%) of the large businesses participated in the OJT program, compared to about one-fourth of the small (28%) and medium-sized (24%) establishments. About three out of 10 firms in central cities (29%), suburbs (26%), and rural/exurban (29%) areas participated in the CETA-OJT program.

• Firms with small proportions of young workers participated in the CETA-OJT program less frequently than firms with high proportions.

Attitudes toward Subminimum Wage Youth Differentials:

• Employers are about evenly divided in their assessment of the impact of a subminimum wage youth differential. While over half (57%) think it will increase jobs for young people, less than half (43%) think it will have no effect (40%) or will decrease (3%) the number of jobs available for young people.
• Trade and service firms are more likely than businesses in other industries to think that a subminimum wage differential will increase jobs for youth. Thus, while a majority of trade and service employers think it will increase jobs for youths, a majority of employers in manufacturing, finance, and "other" businesses do not think it will increase jobs for youths.
• Over half of all businesses surveyed—whether they are small, medium sized, or large—think a subminimum differential will increase jobs for youths. Nevertheless, half of the small (47%) and large (48%) businesses and two-fifths of the medium-sized (40%) firms think that a differential will not increase jobs for young people.

Minority Hiring at Various Wage Subsidies:

• The willingness of employers to hire minority youths is not affected by the level of wage subsidy offered. Regardless of whether they are offered wage subsidies of 50%, 75%, or 100 percent, three out of 10 employers are not willing to hire more minority youth, one out of four are willing, and four out of 10 fail to answer one way or the other.
• Among those employers who answered, they are split about their willingness to hire more minority youths—regardless of the level of wage subsidy offered. Half are willing to hire more minority youths, while the other half are not willing.

Minority Hiring at 100% Wage Subsidy:

• Finance and service firms are more willing to hire minority youths at a 100% wage subsidy than are manufacturing businesses. Six out of 10 finance (61%) and service (57%) firms are willing to hire more minority youths compared to only three out of 10 manufacturing (36%) establishments.
• The willingness of employers to hire more minority youths at a 100% wage subsidy does not vary significantly by size, location, or region of business. But it is directly related to the proportion of teenagers employed. About half of the firms with moderate (61%) and high (54%) proportions of teenage workers are willing to hire more minority youth at a 100% subsidy, compared to only one-third of the businesses with low (36%) proportions of teenage employees.

Job Performance of Youth:

- While six out of 10 employers think that productivity, turnover, and absences among *teenagers* are worse than among mature adults (25 years and older), four out of 10 firms feel that teenagers perform just as well or better than mature adults in those three areas.
- While half of the employers surveyed think that punctuality and discipline among *teenagers* are worse than among mature adults, the other half think that teenagers perform the same or better than mature adults in those two areas.
- More than six out of 10 employers think that the job performance of *young adults* (20-24 years old) was the same or better than that of mature adults (25 years and older) regarding absences, turnover, discipline, punctuality, and productivity, while less than four out of 10 think their performance was worse than that of mature adults in those five areas.

Reasons for Turnover of Youths:

- The two most prevalent reasons for turnover among full-time *teenage* employees in general, which were cited by two-thirds (65%) of the employers surveyed, are quitting (34%) and returning to school (31%).
- The two most prevalent reasons for turnover among full-time *young adult* employees in general, which were cited by about three-fourths (71%) of the employers surveyed, are quitting (44%) and leaving for a better job (27%).
- The main reasons cited for turnover among full-time *minority teenage* employees are quitting, being fired, and leaving for a better job, while the main reasons cited for turnover among full-time *minority young adult* employees are quitting and returning to school.

Ways for Schools to Increase Youth Employability

- The overwhelming majority of employers surveyed place top priority on schools making youth more employable by concentrating on basic reading, writing, and math skills.
- The second most important way that employers felt that schools could increase the employability of young people was by providing them with practical world-of-work orientation.
- The third most important way was by involving private industry in developing work-related school curricula.

Ways for Businesses to Increase Youth Employability

- Employers place highest priority on providing skill training on the job as an effective means for increasing employability of youth.
- The second highest priority was on providing short-term work experience for young people.

- Employers place the lowest priority on creating stronger linkages with job development and placement agencies as a major way for the private sector to increase the employability of youths.

Five-Year Projections for Unskilled Jobs

- The overwhelming majority (84%) of all employers surveyed do not expect the number of unskilled entry-level jobs in their firms to decline over the next five years. Only two out of 10 (17%) expect such a decline, while six out of 10 expect their unskilled jobs to remain the same and one out of four expect them to increase.
- Eight out of 10 manufacturing (88%), service (87%), finance (83%), and trade (81%) firms expect their unskilled jobs to increase or remain the same. Regardless of size, location, or region, most businesses expect no decline in their unskilled jobs.

Five-Year Projections for Semiskilled Jobs

- The overwhelming majority (92%) of employers expect their semiskilled jobs to increase or remain the same over the next five years. One-third (35%) of the employers expect the number of semiskilled jobs in their firms to increase, six out of 10 (57%) expect them to remain the same, and less than one out of 10 (7%) expect them to decline.
- About half of manufacturing, finance, and "other" businesses expect their semiskilled jobs to remain the same, while four out of 10 businesses in those industries expect them to increase.
- Six out of 10 firms—whether small, medium-sized, or large—expect their semiskilled jobs to remain unchanged, while about one-third of them expect them to increase.

Five-Year Projections for Skilled Jobs

- Almost all (94%) of the employers surveyed expect their skilled jobs to increase or remain the same over the next five years. Four out of 10 (43%) firms expect their skilled jobs to increase, half (51%) expect them to remain the same, and only 6% expect them to decline.
- Half of the manufacturing, service, and finance firms expect their skilled jobs to increase, while the other half expect them to remain the same over the next five years.
- The future projections of skilled jobs do not vary by size of business. Four out of 10 employers expect their skilled jobs to increase, whether they are small, medium-sized, or large.

2
An Overview

The Research Objective

The National Urban League Research Department was awarded a grant from the U.S. Department of Labor's Office of Youth Programs to conduct a national survey of private employers' attitudes and practices toward hiring, training, and promoting young people aged 16-24. While the thrust of the survey is on private industry's attitudes and practices toward employment of youths in general, ample attention is also paid to minority youths.

A major question of national concern is, "How can we get private industry to significantly increase opportunities for entry-level employment of young people?" In order to effectively increase private sector jobs for young people in the future, however, it is instructive to have systematic knowledge about past and current experiences and attitudes of employers concerning the performance of young workers.

Although an extensive amount of research has been conducted on numerous aspects of labor market experiences of young people, there are few *nationwide* studies of the attitudes, practices, and policies of private employers toward hiring youths. Much of the research in this area has been based on case studies of only a few firms or on purposively selected companies in a limited number of geographic locations. And no study, for example, has asked national samples of employers about their attitudes toward such controversial topics as subminimum wage differentials and wage subsidies as inducements for hiring young people in general and minority youths in particular.

This study attempts to fill some of these voids by surveying a random cross-section of 535 private employers across the nation during the winter of 1981-82 about the following issues:

1. In which industries and occupations are young people most concentrated?
2. What guidelines are used in hiring young people?

7

3. What opportunities for advancement are provided young workers in private industry?
4. How do employers rate the job performance of youths relative to that of adults?
5. What are the recent hiring patterns of minority youth in private industry?
6. To what extent have private employers participated in major government jobs programs (such as on-the-job training, jobs tax credits, and subminimum-wage youth certificates)?
7. What impact do employers think that a subminimum-wage differential will have on employment opportunities for young people?
8. To what extent would employers be willing to hire more minority youths at wage subsidies of either 100%, 75%, or 50%?
9. What do employers think are the most effective ways for schools and for businesses to increase the employability of young people?
10. What projections do employers have for their unskilled, semi-skilled, and skilled jobs over the next five years?

Thus, the employer survey yields, for the *first time,* comprehensive and nationwide patterns of corporate attitudes and practices toward youths detailed by industry type, size, region, and locale.

Need for Data

The persistent high level of unemployment among young people has increasingly become an issue of vital national concern. Unemployment rates among youths, 16-24 years old, tend to be more than three times higher than the rates for persons 25 years or over. Jobless rates among teenagers are generally five times that of workers 25 years and over, while unemployment rates among those 20-24 years old are about 2.5 times as high.[1]

This problem is especially acute among minority youths whose jobless rates are usually 2 to 3 times higher than that of white youths. In 1982 for instance, the unemployment rates for nonwhite and white male teenagers were about 44% and 22%, respectively, while the jobless rates for nonwhite and white female teenagers were about 44% and 19%, respectively.[2]

In general, the unemployment rates for most young people—even in times of prosperity—continue to be about three times higher than those of the adult labor force. And this persistent high level of joblessness not only deprives these young people of work experience that is needed to enhance their employment opportunities as adults, but it also denies their families of vital income support.[3] Some observers have tried to minimize the seriousness of youth unemployment by claiming that most young people in the labor force (1) are primarily interested in part-time jobs and have only a marginal attachment to the work force, (2) are mostly dropouts and are poorly educated, and (3) are only working for "pin" money and their earnings are not essential for their families. Contrary to popular belief, the majority of young people in the labor force (1) are either employed full time or want full-time jobs, (2) are high school graduates with one-fourth having some college education, and (3) their earnings are vital to the economic well-being of thousands of families, especially among minorities and other low-income groups during periods of high-level inflation and unemployment.[4] Part of the reason for the widespread acceptance of many of these misconceptions about young people is due to the tendency to treat youth as a homogeneous group, when in fact, there are significant differences in work experience, education, and training between various age groups.

Even if one concedes that the chronic high level of unemployment among young people is, in part, due to widespread misconceptions about their work commitments and capabilities, the fundamental issue remains: How do we get more employers, especially in the private sector, to significantly increase the opportunities for meaningful, stable, and regular employment for youths?

An extensive amount of research has been conducted on various aspects of the labor market experience of young people. One of the most extensive investigations has been the National Longitudinal Survey of various age and sex cohorts under the direction of Herbert Parnes at Ohio State University since 1966. Such studies have significantly enhanced our knowledge about various factors that facilitate or inhibit the work mobility of youth.[5]

At the same time, however, there has not been extensive and systematic research on the actual attitudes, practices, and policies of employers with regard to hiring young people. If, indeed, the private sector has unwarranted attitudes, beliefs, and hiring practices regarding young people, it is imperative that the nature and extent of such beliefs and practices be systematically identified and documented in order to develop meaningful programmatic actions to counteract any misinformation. On the other hand, a comprehensive study of private industry may reveal that many attitudes and practices on the part of employers toward youth are quite valid and reliable, and thus may require governmental actions and programs that remove various barriers for employers to hire young people.

Sample and Methods

This survey is based on the replies of 535 employment officials to a questionnaire that was mailed to 5,000 business establishments across the nation. Thus, about 10% of the establishments surveyed responded to the questionnaire. The Equal Employment Opportunity Commission Employer Information Report (EEO-1) list was used to select the sample. This list was used for a number of reasons: (1) its cost

TABLE 2.1
SAMPLE CHARACTERISTICS

Characteristic	Number in Sample
Establishment Type	
Manufacturing	88
Trade	137
Finance	49
Service	158
Other[a]	40
Not determined	63
Total	535
Number of Employees	
Less than 100	102
250-249	244
250 and over	171
Not determined	18
Total	535
Location	
Central cities/towns	270
Suburbs	156
Rural/Exurbs	88
Not determined	21
Total	535
Region	
Northeast	100
North Central	163
Northwest	97
South	150
Not determined	25
Total	535

a. Other establishments include agriculture, mining, construction, and transportation. These businesses were collapsed into a single category because the percentage of businesses reporting in these categories was relatively small.

compared to other available lists; (2) its reasonably good coverage of most industries compared to other lists; (3) its manageable size; (4) the familiarity of EEO-1 respondents with retrieval of employment data; and (5) the EEO-1 data file provided the address and phone number of persons familiar with data retrieval, thus potentially enhancing the response rate. (See Appendix A for a detailed discussion of the EEO-1 universe list.)

To insure that establishments of various sizes and types were represented in the sample, a stratified random sampling procedure was used to create two strata of establishments, one with 100 or more employees and the other with less than 100. Industries were clustered into four groups using the Standard Industrial Classification (SIC) code—(1) manufacturing, (2) trade, (3) service, and (4) agriculture, mining, construction, transportation, and finance.

The use of stratification was intended to make the sample more efficient by establishing eight strata that were internally homogeneous regarding industry and size groupings. These strata were sampled in proportion to their sizes to insure the required range of industry types and sizes in the sample. (See Appendix B for a full description of the sampling plan.)

The answers to the questionnaire reflected the perspective of a single plant/establishment or a branch of a business with several locations. Thus, if a business had multiple branches, the questionnaire was filled out at the particular site where the questionnaire was received. (See questionnaire in Appendix C.)

The characteristics of the surveyed business establishments by type, size, location, and region are shown in Table 2.1.

Notes

1. Walter E. Williams, "Youth and Minority Unemployment," prepared for the U.S. Congress Joint Economic Committee (U.S. Government Printing Office, Washington, D.C., July 6, 1977).
2. These are annual averages of unadjusted unemployment rates for 1982 (Office of Employment Analysis, Bureau of Labor Statistics, U.S. Dept. of Labor, 1982).
3. National Child Labor Committee, *Rites of Passage: The Crisis of Youth's Transition from School to Work* (New York: National Child Labor Committee, 1976).
4. Robert B. Hill, *The Illusion of Black Progress* (Washington, D.C., NUL Research Development, 1978); Diane N. Westcott, "Youth in the Labor Force: An Area Study," *Monthly Labor Review*, U.S. Bureau of Labor Statistics (July 1976), pp. 3-9.
5. Andrew I. Kohen and Herbert S. Parnes, *Career Thresholds: A Longitudinal Study of the Educational and Labor Market Experience of Male Youth* (Columbus, Oh.: Center for Human Resources Research, Ohio State University, June 1971, vol. 3); Paul Bullock, *Youth in the Labor Market: Employment Patterns and Career Aspirations in Watts and East Los Angeles*, prepared for U.S. Department of Labor Manpower Administration (January 1972).

3
Representation of Youths in the Private Sector and Hiring Guidelines

The description of the industrial and occupational representation of youths in the private labor market in this chapter is based on employers' estimates of the proportion of youth workers—high, moderate, and low—in the workplace. We also profile the hiring guidelines used by the national sample of business establishments in the NUL survey.

Industry Representation

Where are young workers, aged 16-24, concentrated in the private labor force? What types of firms tend to employ them? Are young employees found more often in small businesses than in large businesses? What are the differences in employment patterns of teenagers, aged 16-19, and young adults, aged 20-24? These questions are addressed in this section in an attempt to describe the representation of young workers in private industry. First, we look at the proportions of the teenagers, aged 16-19, hired in all businesses, followed by profiles of the proportion of all teenagers employed based on type of business and size of business. Second, we outline the proportions of young adults, aged 20-24, hired in all businesses, and describe the proportion of young adults employed by type of and size of business.

Teenage Workers, Aged 16-19

Proportion Employed by All Establishments. Firms were asked to estimate the percentage of teenagers, aged 16-19, in their respective workforces. These percentages were collapsed into three approximately equal-sized groups that indicated whether their proportion of teenage hires was "high" (10% or more) "moderate" (2-9%), or "low" (0-1%). Figure 3.1 reveals that 31% of the establishments estimate that teenage employees constitute a low proportion (0-1%) of their total workforce. Similarly, 32% report a moderate (2-9%) proportion and slightly more than a third (36%) estimate that teen hires comprise a high proportion (10% or more) of the total workforce.

FIGURE 3.1
ESTIMATED PROPORTION OF TEENAGERS EMPLOYED,
BY ALL BUSINESSES

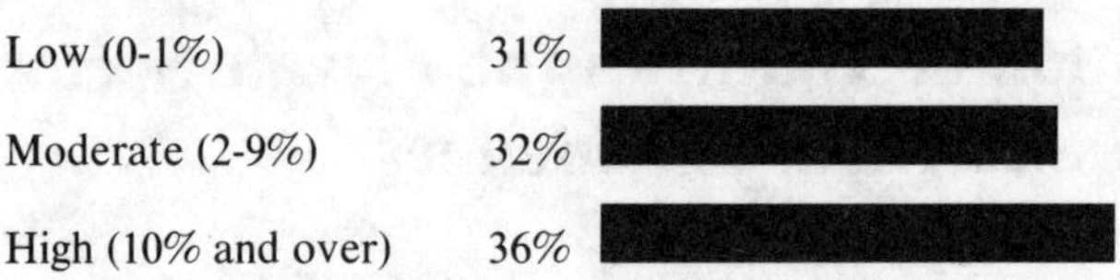

Low (0-1%)	31%	▮▮▮▮▮▮▮▮▮▮
Moderate (2-9%)	32%	▮▮▮▮▮▮▮▮▮▮
High (10% and over)	36%	▮▮▮▮▮▮▮▮▮▮▮

Note: Percentages may not add to 100 due to rounding.

Business Type. As might be expected, employment patterns of teenagers, aged 16-19,[1] varies by type of business. Trade establishments employ the highest proportion of teenagers, aged 16-19. In three-fifths (60%) of the trade establishments, teenagers are 10% or more of the workforce. Service and finance businesses rank second in hiring teenager workers. In about a third (35%) of the service establishments, and in 29% of the finance establishments, teenagers are 10% or more of the workforce. By contrast, manufacturing and "other" businesses (agriculture, mining, construction, transportation) rank lowest in employing teenagers. In only one-fifth (18%) of the manufacturing concerns and in only 13% of "other" businesses are teenagers 10% or more of the workplace (see Table 3.1).

Business Size. Unexpectedly, employers' estimates of the proportion of teenagers employed do not vary appreciably by size of business. For example, teenage workers comprise 10% or more of the workforce in 40% of small (1-99) businesses, 35% of medium-sized (100-249) businesses, and 37% of large (250 or more employees) businesses. Conversely, teenage hires constitute low proportions (1% or less) of the workforce in 36% of small businesses, 29% of medium-sized business, and 32% of large businesses (see Table 3.2).

Young Adult Workers, Aged 20-24

Proportion Employed by All Establishments. Employers were also asked to estimate the percentage of young adults, aged 20-24, in their workforces. These estimates were also combined into three groups to indicate whether firms have a "high" (25% and over), "moderate" (15-24%), or "low" (0-14%) proportion of young adults in the workplace. Figure 3.2 shows that 32% of the firms report low (0-14%) proportions of young adult hires, while nearly three out of 10 (28%) report moder-

TABLE 3.1
**ESTIMATED PROPORTION OF TEENAGERS EMPLOYED,
BY TYPE OF BUSINESS**

Proportion Employed	Business				
	Manufacturing	Trade	Finance	Service	Other[a]
Low (0-1%)	41	16	33	30	65
Moderate (2-9%)	41	24	39	35	23
High (10% and over)	18	60	29	35	13
Total	100	100	100	100	100
Sample Size	(88)	(137)	(49)	(158)	(40)

a. Other businesses include agriculture, mining, construction, and transportation.
Note: Percentages may not add to 100 due to rounding.

TABLE 3.2
ESTIMATED PROPORTION OF TEENAGERS EMPLOYED,
BY SIZE OF BUSINESS

	Size		
Proportion Employed	Small (1-99)	Medium (100-249)	Large (250 & over)
Low (0-1%)	36	29	32
Moderate (2-9%)	24	37	31
High (10% and over)	40	35	37
Total	100	100	100
Sample Size	(87)	(229)	(156)

Note: Percentages may not add to 100 due to rounding.

ate proportions (15-24%) and four out of 10 (40%) report high proportions (25% or more) of young adult hires in their workforces.

Business Type. As with teenage workers, type of business is related to employers' estimates of the proportion of young adult hires. As shown in Table 3.3, finance, trade, and service establishments employ the highest proportions of young adult workers. Young adults comprise 25% or more of the total workforce in half (51%) of the finance businesses, in 45% of the trade establishments, and in 41% of the service businesses. On the other hand, in only three-tenths (31%) of manufacturing and "other" (30%) businesses do young adults constitute 25% or more of the total workforce.

Business Size. Following the same trend as for teenage hires, size of business does not vary significantly with the proportion of young adult workers. As revealed in Table 3.4, young adults make up 25% or more of the workplace in approximately four out of 10 businesses regardless of whether they are small (41%), medium (37%), or large (44%). On the other hand, young adult hires comprise a low proportion (14% or less) in about one out of three businesses regardless of size.

Occupational Representation

In what occupations are young workers most concentrated in private industry? That is to say, what job positions do youths typically hold?

FIGURE 3.2
ESTIMATED PROPORTION OF YOUNG ADULTS EMPLOYED,
BY ALL BUSINESSES

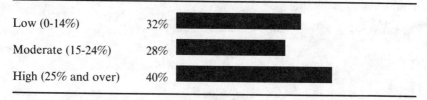

Low (0-14%)   32%

Moderate (15-24%) 28%

High (25% and over) 40%

Note: Percentages may not add to 100 due to rounding.

TABLE 3.3
ESTIMATED PROPORTION OF YOUNG ADULTS EMPLOYED,
BY TYPE OF BUSINESS

	Business				
Proportion Employed	Manufacturing	Trade	Finance	Service	Other[a]
Low (0-1%)	40	27	22	32	48
Moderate (2-9%)	30	29	27	27	23
High (10% and over)	31	45	51	41	30
Total	100	100	100	100	100
Sample Size	(27)	(61)	(25)	(65)	(12)

a. Other businesses include agriculture, mining, construction, and transportation.
Note: Percentages may not add to 100 due to rounding.

Figure 3.3 reflects what has been already documented about industries: clerical, sales, laborer, and service jobs are most likely to be the province of young workers.[2] For example, teenage hires, aged 16-19, typically occupy service (28%), clerical (25%), and laborer (22%) positions. Thus, three-fourths of all teenage workers are clustered around the lower end of the occupational ladder. Young adult hires, aged 20-24, though, hold a slight advantage in the upper rungs of the ladder. While one-fifth (20%) hold professional, managerial, and technical positions, young adults are also dominant in clerical (23%) and service (21%) jobs. On the other hand, the figures also reveal an

FIGURE 3.3
POSITIONS YOUTHS TYPICALLY OCCUPY

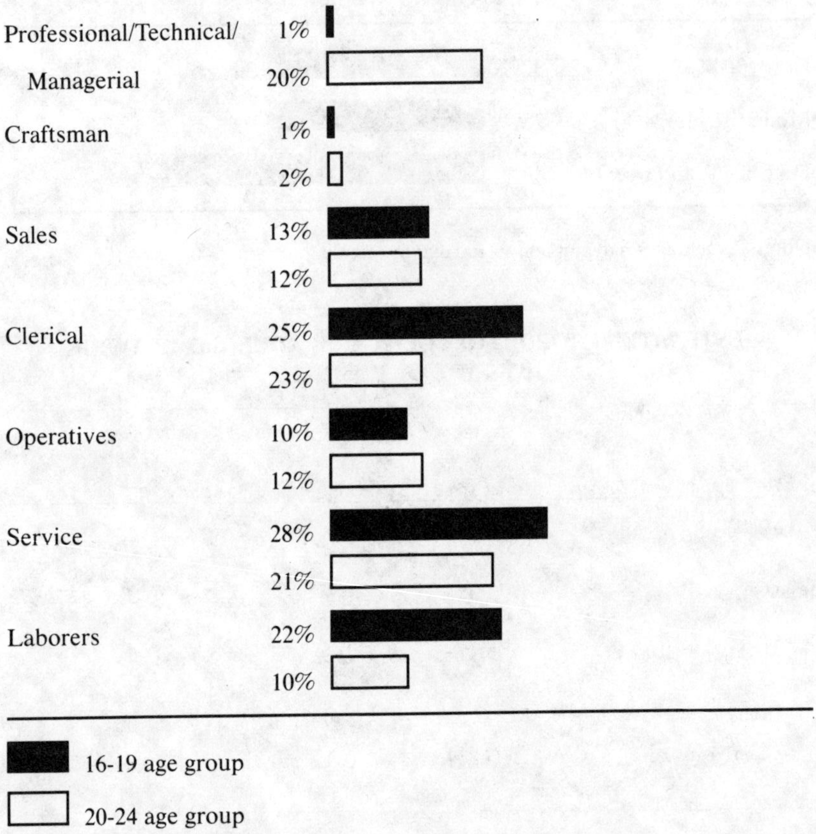

Professional/Technical/	1%
Managerial	20%
Craftsman	1%
	2%
Sales	13%
	12%
Clerical	25%
	23%
Operatives	10%
	12%
Service	28%
	21%
Laborers	22%
	10%

■ 16-19 age group

□ 20-24 age group

Note: Percentages may not add to 100 due to rounding.

underrepresentation of young adults in craftsman (2%), sales (12%), and operative (12%) jobs.

Business Type

To what extent does the occupational distribution of teenagers and young adults vary by type of establishment? For simplicity's sake, we employed a dichotomous classification of occupations—blue collar and white collar.[3]

The results in Table 3.5 indicate that occupations vary by type of firm for both age groups of youths. For example, three-fourths or more

TABLE 3.4
ESTIMATED PROPORTION OF YOUNG ADULTS EMPLOYED,
BY SIZE OF BUSINESS

	Size		
Proportion Employed	Small (1-99)	Medium (100-249)	Large (250 & over)
Low (0-14%)	31	31	35
Moderate (15-24%)	28	32	21
High (25% and over)	41	37	44
Total	100	100	100
Sample Size	(87)	(229)	(156)

Note: Percentages may not add to 100 due to rounding.

of teenage employees are in blue-collar jobs in manufacturing (87%), service (77%), and "other" (74%), businesses, while over half hold white-collar jobs in trade (54%) and finance (90%) firms. Similarly, over half of all young adult employees hold blue-collar jobs in manufacturing (70%), service (52%), and "other" (56%) business, while over two-thirds hold white-collar jobs in trade (71%) and finance (87%) establishments. Thus, the occupations that young employees typically occupy by type of establishment are similar for both teenagers and young adult workers.

Hiring Guidelines

What do companies look for in hiring entry-level employees? Previous research indicates that getting a job is based on both formal and informal standards. Formal or "objective" standards usually include education and prior work experience. For certain jobs, age and level of skill training may also be determinants. By contrast, informal standards rely on subjective criteria, such as willingness to work, other work-related attitudes, style of dress, and communication skills.[4]

The education standard for entry-level jobs translates into the ability to read and write. For most firms, especially the larger ones, the high school diploma is a minimum requirement in obtaining employment.[5]

TABLE 3.5
ESTIMATED PERCENTAGE OF JOBS YOUTHS TYPICALLY HOLD, BY TYPE OF BUSINESS

| | Business | | | | | | | | | |
Job Type	Manufacturing		Trade		Finance		Service		Other [a]	
	Teenagers	Young Adults	Teenagers	Young Adults	Teenagers	Young Adults	Teenagers	Young Adults	Teenagers	Young Adults
White Collar	13	30	54	71	90	87	23	48	26	44
Blue Collar	87	70	46	29	11	13	77	52	74	56
Total	100	100	100	100	100	100	100	100	100	100
Sample Size	(72)	(83)	(122)	(130)	(45)	(47)	(137)	(144)	(29)	(78)

a. Other businesses include agriculture, mining, construction, and transportation.
Note: Percentages may not add to 100 due to rounding.

Sometimes the educational requirement exceeds the job task. Prior work experience, too, is strongly related to securing a job. Ironically a major barrier to young people getting work is not having *had* a job. Large employers, in particular, often want to employ "proven commodities." And, for some jobs, *directly* relevant work experience is needed along with credentialed skill training.[6]

In terms of informal requirements for entry-level positions, large and small employers seek individuals with a willingness to work hard, follow directions, and possessing "maturity."[7] Style of dress and speech patterns, too, are subjective criteria that affect youth employment. Inappropriate dress and nonstandard English also act as deterrents for hiring youths.[8]

To determine the nature of hiring policies for young employees, the NUL survey asked employers whether their companies used any of the following guidelines in hiring teenage and young adult workers:

• Hire for unskilled jobs.
• Hire for part-time jobs.
• Hire for entry-level jobs.
• Hire those with experience.
• Hire for any job not prohibited by child labor laws.

The greatest differences in hiring guidelines for both age groups relate to: (1) hiring for part-time jobs, (2) hiring for entry-level jobs, and (3) hiring those with experience. Hiring guidelines for part-time jobs among the businesses surveyed favor teenagers. Three-fourths (75%) of the business have guidelines for part-time work for hiring teenagers, compared to 60% with guidelines for hiring young adults for part-time jobs. On the other hand, hiring for entry-level jobs favors young adult workers. Eight out of 10 (82%) have guidelines for hiring young adults in entry-level jobs, compared to only six out of 10 (58%) establishments with guidelines for hiring teenagers for entry positions. Guidelines for hiring youths with experience favor young adults. About eight out of 10 (84%) firms have guidelines for hiring young adults with experience in contrast to only four out of 10 (39%) that employ work experience guidelines for hiring teenagers (see Figure 3.4).

Summary of Findings

Industrial Representation

• Young adults, aged 20-24 years, are hired in private industry to a much greater extent than teenagers, aged 16-19 years. In about two-

FIGURE 3.4
HIRING GUIDELINES FOR YOUNG WORKERS

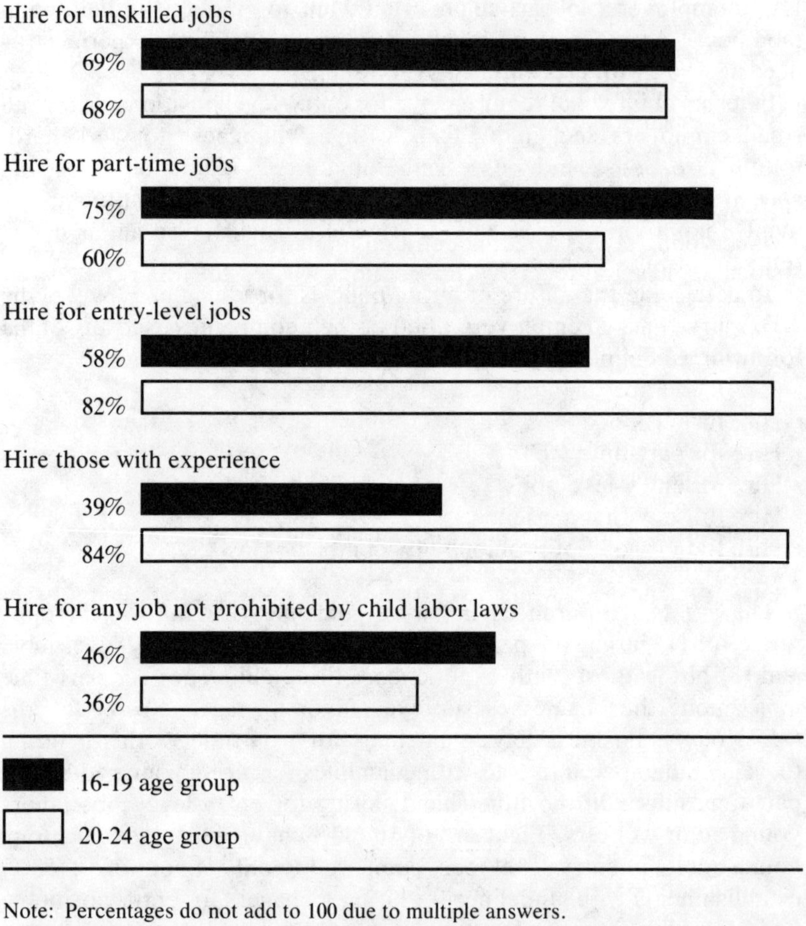

Hire for unskilled jobs

69%

68%

Hire for part-time jobs

75%

60%

Hire for entry-level jobs

58%

82%

Hire those with experience

39%

84%

Hire for any job not prohibited by child labor laws

46%

36%

■ 16-19 age group

□ 20-24 age group

Note: Percentages do not add to 100 due to multiple answers.

fifths of all businesses surveyed, teenagers comprise at least one-tenth of all employees, while young adults account for at least one-fourth of all employees.

• Teenagers and young adults are concentrated in the same industries. Teenagers account for 10% or more of all employees in 60% of trade, 35% of service, and 29% of finance businesses, compared to only 18% of manufacturing and 13% of "other" (i.e., agriculture, mining, construction, and transportation) establishments. Young adults make up 25% or more of all employees in 45% of trade, 41% of service, and

51% of finance firms, compared to only 31% of manufacturing and 30% of "other" businesses.

- The proportion of young workers hired in private industry does not vary by size of business. Teenagers comprise at least one-tenth of all employees in about two-fifths of small (40%), medium (35%), or large (37%) businesses. Similarly, young adults account for at least one-fourth of all employees in about two-fifths of small (41%), medium (37%), or large (44%) businesses.

Occupational Representation

- Teenagers are concentrated in clerical, service, and laborer jobs, while young adults are concentrated in clerical, service, and professional/managerial/technical occupations. Three-fourths (75%) of all teenagers are employed as clerical workers (25%), service workers (28%), and laborers (27%), while about two-thirds (64%) of all young adults are employed as clerical workers (23%), service workers (21%), and professional/managerial/technical workers (20%).
- Teenagers and young adults have similar occupational-industrial patterns. Over three-fourths of teenage employees hold blue-collar jobs in manufacturing (87%), service (77%), and "other" (74%) industries, while over half hold white-collar jobs in trade (54%) and finance (90%) firms. Similarly, over half of all young adult employees hold blue-collar jobs in manufacturing (70%), service (52%), and "other" (56%) businesses, while over two-thirds hold white-collar jobs in trade (71%) and finance (87%) establishments.

Hiring Guidelines

- Private businesses use hiring guidelines that vary for teenagers and young adults.
- Young adults are more likely than teenagers to be hired for entry-level positions. Four-fifths (82%) of all businesses hire young adults for entry-level jobs, while only 58% of them hire teenagers for such jobs.
- Young adults are more likely than teenagers to be hired for jobs that require some experience. Four-fifths (84%) of all businesses hire young adults for occupations requiring experience, while only two-fifths (39%) hire teenagers for such posts.
- However, teenagers are more likely than young adults to be hired for part-time positions. Three-fourths (75%) of all businesses hire teens for part-time jobs, while only 60% of them hire young adults for such jobs.
- Teenagers are also more likely than young adults to be hired for jobs not prohibited by child labor laws. About half (46%) of all businesses hire teenagers for such jobs, while 36% hire young adults.
- Teenagers and young adults are equally likely to be hired for un-

skilled jobs. About two-thirds of all businesses hire teenagers (69%) or young adults (68%) for unskilled positions.

Notes

1. More specifically, previous research has documented that the biggest single employer of youths is the nondurable retail trade sector because these are jobs in clothing stores, grocery stores, and gas stations, for example, which require little knowledge of the product. See Marcia Freedman, "The Youth Labor Market" in *From School to Work: Improving the Transition* (Washington, D.C.: National Commission for Manpower Policy, 1976), p. 27.
2. Ibid., p. 27
3. Blue-collar occupations were defined as craftsmen, operatives, service, and laborers. White-collar occupations were defined as professional/technical/managerial, sales, and clerical.
4. Daniel E. Diamond and Hrach Bedrosian, *Industry Hiring Requirements and Employment of Disadvantaged Groups* (New York: New York University School of Commerce, 1970). Edith F. Lynton et al., *Employer's Views on Hiring and Training* (New York: Labor Market Information, 1978). Erik Butler and James Darr, *Research on Youth Employment and Employability Development: Educator and Employer Perspectives* (Massachusetts: Brandeis University, May 1980), p. 19.
5. National Commission for Manpower Policy, "Corporate Hiring Practices," in *From School to Work: Improving the Transition* (Washington, D.C.: National Commission for Manpower Policy, 1976), p. 39.
6. Butler and Darr, pp. 19, 24.
7. Ibid., p. 19
8. Diamond and Bedrosian; Edith F. Lynton et al.

4
Advancement Opportunities
for Young Employees

To what extent do young people have access to jobs with advancement opportunities? Clearly, the preponderant evidence from other research reveals that youth, by and large, are excluded from jobs with advancement potential or career opportunities until the age of 20 or 21.[1] Indeed, research on accessibility of career-type jobs for youth indicate that employers were less desirous of young people under 21 than older youth when jobs with clear lines of progression were at stake or, as Diamond and Bedrosian termed it, there existed an availability of "families of jobs."[2]

A notable exception to the evidence that youths are generally excluded from access to entry-level jobs with career potential is a study of three large companies—manufacturing, utilities, and retail trade—conducted by the National Commission for Manpower Policy.[3] The investigators found that a substantial proportion of new young workers were hired into jobs with clear and recognized lines of progression. They concluded that opportunities for training and advancement for the young worker depend, to some extent, on whether the job is seasonal, part time, or full-time with no advancement potential.

Another line of thinking is that entry level jobs, per se, should not be viewed as "dead ends." The fact that some companies use job posting and personnel data banks to foster internal development "can make a difference between a dead end or a stepping stone."[4] Although some business establishments may follow this practice, the fate of young workers, particularly minority youths, is tied to the ebb and flow of economic conditions and to the degree to which companies adhere to federal policies for protected groups.[5]

The NUL survey asked firms to describe the extent to which advancement opportunities are available for young workers in the positions where they are *most* concentrated. We asked the question this way in order to generalize about advancement opportunities for *most* young hires based on employer characteristics of business type and size. Although the assessment of advancement opportunities is a complicated notion and depends upon such factors as seniority systems, unionization, promotion policies, and opportunities for skill training, the firms' perceptions of overall upgrading opportunities for youths are considered important. We will now seek answers to the following questions: Does advancement opportunity for youths vary with type of business? Is size of business related to advancement opportunities for youths?

Business Type

Advancement opportunities for youth hires do vary with the type of firm. Trade firms tend of offer the greatest amount of advancement for teenagers while service establishments offer the least advancement. One-third (34%) of trade businesses report "a great extent" of advancement opportunities, compared to only 16% of service businesses. About one-fourth of the manufacturing (25%), finance (29%), and "other" (28%) businesses also report "a great extent" of advancement opportunities for teenagers.

However, with regard to young adults, trade and finance firms offer the greatest mobility options. Three-fifths of the businesses in trade (59%) and finance (57%) report "a great extent" of advancement opportunities for young adults, compared to about one-third of service (31%), manufacturing (37%), and "other" (35%) businesses (see Table 4.1).

Business Size

Opportunities for advancement also vary with size of business. Interestingly, advancement opportunities for young workers are more available in small (1-99) than in medium (100-249) or large (250 employees more) companies. Two-fifths (39%) of small businesses report "a great extent" of advancement options for teenage workers compared to about one-fourth of large (25%) and medium-sized (21%) businesses. Similarly, 55% of small firms offer "a great extent" of mobility opportunities for young adults, compared to two-fifths of large (41%) and medium-sized (41%) firms (see Table 4.2).

Summary of Findings

Advancement Opportunities for Youths

• Young workers have the most opportunities for advancement in trade and finance industries and the least opportunities in service firms.

TABLE 4.1
ADVANCEMENT OPPORTUNITIES FOR YOUTHS,
BY TYPE OF BUSINESS
(PERCENTAGE DISTRIBUTION)

Advancement Opportunities	Manufacturing		Trade		Business Finance		Service		Other [a]	
	Teenagers	Young Adults	Teenagers	Young Adults	Teenagers	Young Adults	Teenagers	Young Adults	Teenagers	Young Adults
A Great Extent	25	37	34	59	29	57	16	31	28	35
Some	47	49	47	38	56	43	44	47	31	50
Very Little/None	29	13	19	4	16	-[b]	40	22	41	15
Total	100	100	100	100	100	100	100	100	100	100
Sample Size	(72)	(83)	(122)	(130)	(45)	(47)	(137)	(144)	(29)	(78)

a. Other businesses include mining, agriculture, construction and transportation.
b. There were no answers in this category.
Note: Percentages may not add to 100 due to rounding.

TABLE 4.2
ADVANCEMENT OPPORTUNITIES FOR YOUNG EMPLOYEES, BY SIZE OF BUSINESS
(PERCENTAGE DISTRIBUTION)

Advancement Opportunities	Size					
	Small (1-99)		Medium (100-249)		Large (250 & over)	
	Teenagers	Young Adults	Teenagers	Young Adults	Teenagers	Young Adults
A Great Extent	39	55	21	41	25	41
Some	41	39	47	43	47	50
Very Little/None	20	6	32	16	29	9
Total	100	100	100	100	100	100
Sample Size	(74)	(78)	(202)	(220)	(129)	(140)

Note: Percentages may not add to 100 due to rounding.

Eight out of 10 trade (81%) and finance (85%) businesses surveyed reported that they provide "some" or "a great extent" of advancement options for teenagers, compared to only six out of 10 service (60%) and "other" (59%) establishments. Similarly, almost all of the trade (96%) and finance (99%) business have advancement opportunities for young adults, compared to only two-thirds (68%) of the service firms.

• Teenagers tend to have greater advancement opportunities in small (50-99 employees) rather than medium-sized (100-249 employees) or large (250 or more employees) businesses. Eight out of 10 small business provide advancement opportunities for teenagers, compared to seven out of 10 medium-sized (68%) and large (71%) establishments.

• However, young adults tend to have more advancement chances in small and large businesses than in medium-sized ones. Over nine-tenths of the small (94%) and large (91%) businesses provide advancement opportunities for young adults, compared to 85% of the medium-sized firms.

Notes

1. Paul E. Barton, "Youth Employment and Career Entry," in Seymour L. Wolfbein, ed., *Labor Market Information for Youths* (Philadelphia: Temple University Press, 1975), p. 87.
2. Ibid., p. 91.
3. National Commission for Manpower Policy, "Corporate Hiring Practices," in *From School to Work: Improving the Transition* (Washington, D.C.: National Commission for Manpower Policy, 1976), p. 39.
4. Edith F. Lynton et al., *Employers' Views on Hiring and Training* (New York: Labor Market Information Network, 1978), p. 263.
5. Robert B. Hill, "Discrimination and Minority Youth Unemployment," in *A Review of Youth Employment Programs and Policies* (Washington: Vice-President's Task Force on Youth Employment, 1980); Robert M. Solow, "Employment Policy in Inflationary Times," in Eli Ginzberg, ed., *Employing the Unemployed* (New York: Basic Books, 1980), pp. 129-41; National Manpower Institute, *Study of Corporate Youth Employment Policies and Practices* (Washington, D.C.: National Manpower Institute, 1973).

5
Industry's Attitudes
toward Young Workers

Many experts hold that attitudes toward work play a major role in the labor market experiences of young people. The underlying premise is that positive work attitudes are associated with stable and successful employment patterns among youth, while negative attitudes have harmful effects on finding a job and adjustment to work. The empirical evidence to confirm this hypothesis has been, at times, supportive and, at other times, nonsupportive.[1]

Regardless of the empirical relationship between the work attitudes of youth and their employment experiences, however, the bulk of employers in past studies view young peoples' "attitudes" as a major barrier to hiring more of them. Many employers characterize most youths as having negative attitudes toward the value of work,[2] being unstable, irresponsible,[3] lacking motivation, having poor work performance, and high absenteeism[4]—especially disadvantaged youths.[5] One report went so far as to say that employers' negative views toward youth were "connected with a general antipathy to the young."[6]

Large employers, in particular, identified discipline among young workers as a major concern. Poor discipline was viewed as a major cause for most terminations. Many youths, the larger employers contend, view the "behavioral prescriptives" of the workplace as a "personal affront"—an indication that they do not understand the structure of the work organization.[7] Thus, many studies reveal that major employers, by and large, tend to favor workers 21 years and older.[8]

Many employers insist that job training programs for youth should focus on proper work attitudes and habits to enhance the assimilation of young people into the world of work.[9] Although recent quasi-experimental studies examined the impact of employment and training programs on the work attitudes of youths, their findings are far from conclusive. Several studies conclude that youths participating in job

31

training programs do not differ significantly from control groups on a number of job-holding skills, job knowledge, and work-relevant attitudes.[10] On the other hand, other research reports significant, measurable gains by job-training participants compared to nonparticipants on tests of work-related attitudes and job-seeking skills.[11] While attitude gains did not increase success in job finding they were associated with slightly higher status jobs.[12]

Again, on the positive side, a study by Greenleigh Associates reported that youth employees from a JOBS training program performed as well as adult hires, and that absenteeism was less pronounced among JOBS participants than among the regular hires.[13] Another study on corporate hiring practices found that, in general, there were no major differences between young employees and adult workers regarding on-the-job performance.[14] Furthermore, a study of business attitudes toward CETA revealed that approximately seven out of 10 private employees surveyed did *not* have serious problems with the attendance and motivation of trainees from CETA on-the-job programs. And nearly eight out of 10 employers did *not* experience serious problems with CETA trainees in off-the-job programs.[15]

Results of NUL Employer Survey

Our survey assessed employer attitudes toward young workers concerning the following frequently cited criteria of performance: punctuality, retention, absence, productivity, discipline, and training costs.[16] We also wanted to determine whether businesses' attitudes toward young workers vary for different age groups. We will now examine private-sector attitudes toward youths ages 16-19 and 20-24 on a number of work-related attributes.

Punctuality. About half (52%) of the establishments rated the punctuality of teenage workers *poorer* than for adult employees 25 and over, while only one-fourth (27%) rated the punctuality of young adult workers as *poorer* than adult employees 25 and over. Nevertheless, half (49%) of the employers said that teenagers were just as or more punctual than adult workers (see Figure 5.1).

Retention. Three-fifths (61%) of the businesses rated the retention of teenager hires as *poorer* than adult employees compared to one-third (35%) that rated the retention of young adult hires as *poorer* than adult workers 25 and over.

Absences. Six out of 10 (61%) of the businesses reported that teenager hires have *more* absences than adult employees aged 25 and

FIGURE 5.1
A COMPARISON OF YOUNG EMPLOYEES WITH ADULTS ON
WORK-RELATED ATTRIBUTES

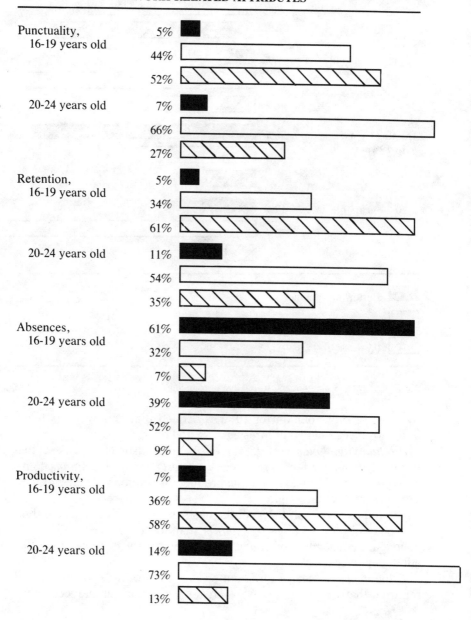

FIGURE 5.1 (cont.)

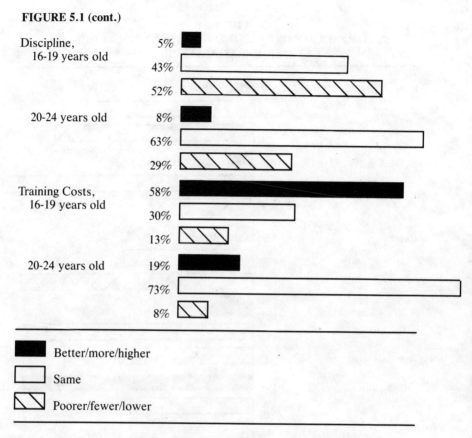

Note: Percentages may not add to 100 due to rounding.

over, while only four out of 10 (39%) stated that young adults have *more* absences than adult hires aged 25 and over.

Productivity. Over half (58%) of the establishments ranked the productivity of teenage employees as *poorer* than adult hires, compared to only 13% that ranked the productivity of young adult workers as *poorer* than adult employees.

Discipline. Over half (52%) of the businesses surveyed reported that discipline of teenage hires was *poorer* than for adult hires, while 29% believed the discipline of young adult employees was *poorer* than for adult employees.

Training costs. Nearly three out of five (58%) of the establishments reported that training costs were *higher* for teenage employees compared to adult hires, while one in five (19%) stated that training costs for young adult hires were *higher* than for adult employees 25 and over.

Based on these data, the establishments did not perceive young workers as monolithically "unstable," "irresponsible," or "unredeemable." Evidently, young adult hires, aged 20-24, are regarded almost as productive as adult employees. By contrast, over half of the establishments rated the performance of teenage hires, 16-19 years old, as worse than the performance of adult workers aged 25 and over. Thus, as young workers mature, chronologically, businesses' attitudes toward them grow more positive on all performance criteria.

The Turnover Rate

Youths in General

What factors contribute most to the turnover rate among full-time young employees? The national sample of companies was requested to check the *one* factor that contributed most to the turnover rate among both age groups of youths with full-time positions. For full-time *teenage employees,* over one-third of the firms reported that "quitting or resigning" (38%) and "returning to school" (34%) were the most prevalent reasons for turnover. For full-time *young adult* workers, nearly half (48%) of the employers stated that "quitting or resigning" was the most prevalent reason for turnover within this age group. The second most prevalent reason for turnover was "leaving for a better job" (29%) (see Figure 5.2).

Minority Youths

Twenty-seven companies among the surveyed establishments had special jobs programs for minority youths. These employers were asked to check the main cause of turnover among minority teenagers and young adults who participated in their company's jobs programs. For minority teenagers, aged 16-19, 11 of the firms cited "quitting or resigning" as the most prevalent reason for turnover. Seven of the establishments cited "firing or dismissal" for turnover; five stated "leaving for a better job;" and only one cited "returning to school." For minority young adults, aged 20-24, nine firms reported "quitting or resigning" and eight firms cited "returning to school" as the most prevalent reasons for turnover. Only three companies reported "summer or temporary employment" as the main cause of turnover among minority young adults.

FIGURE 5.2
REASONS FOR TURNOVER AMONG FULL-TIME YOUNG EMPLOYEES

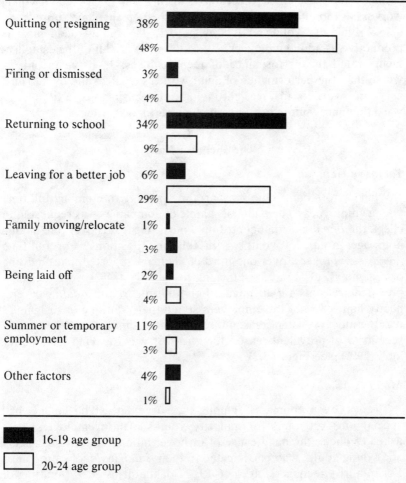

▪	16-19 age group
▫	20-24 age group

Summary of Findings

Job Performance of Youths

• Six out of 10 businesses surveyed think that the job performance of *teenagers* is worse than that of mature adults (25 years and older) regarding productivity (58%), turnover (61%), and absences (61%). Nevertheless, four out of 10 firms feel that teenagers perform just as well or better than mature adults in those three areas.

• Businesses are divided in their perceptions of the performance of *teenagers* relative to mature adults regarding punctuality (52%) and

discipline (52%). Half of them feel that teenagers perform worse than adults in these two areas, while the other half feel that they perform the same or better than adults.
- No less than six out of 10 firms feel that the job performance of *young adults* (20-24 years old) was the same or better than that of mature adults (25 years and over) regarding absences (61%), turnover (65%), discipline (71%), punctuality (73%), and productivity (87%), while less than four out of 10 think that their performance was worse than that of mature adults in those five areas.

Reasons for Turnover of Youth

- The two most prevalent reasons for turnover among full-time *teenage* employees in general cited by two-thirds (65%) of the businesses surveyed are quitting (38%) and returning to school (34%). Only one-tenth of the firms feel that the main reasons for turnover are due to being laid off (2%), fired (3%), or leaving for a better job (6%).
- The two most prevalent reasons for turnover among full-time *young adult* employees in general cited by three-fourths (77%) of the businesses surveyed are quitting (48%) and leaving for a better job (29%). Less than one-fifth (15%) of the businesses cited returning to school (9%), being laid off (4%), and being fired (4%) as the main reasons for turnover among young adult workers.
- Concerning minority youths, the main reasons cited for turnover among full-time *teenage* employees are quitting, being fired, or leaving for a better job.
- Concerning minority youths, the main reasons cited for turnover among full-time *young adult* employees are quitting and returning to school.

Notes

1. Youth Programs, "Do Work Attitudes Matter" (Massachusetts: Brandeis University Press, Center for Employment and Income Studies, 1982), p. 13.
2. Erik Butler and James Darr, *Research on Youth Employment and Employability Development: Educator and Employer Perspectives* (Massachusetts: Brandeis University Press, 1980), p. 22.
3. Eli Cohen et al., *Getting Hired, Getting Trained: A Study of Industry Practices and Policies on Youth Employment* (Washington, D.C.: U.S. Government Printing Office, 1965), p. 19.
4. The White House, *A Summary Report of the Vice-President's Task Force on Youth Employment* (Washington, D.C.: The White House, 1980).
5. David Robison, ed., *Small Business Employment and the Work Preparation of Youth* (Washington, D.C.: The Vice-President's Task Force on Youth Employment, 1979).
6. Cohen et al., p. 88.
7. Butler and Darr, p. 25.
8. Daniel E. Diamond and Hrach Bedrosian, *Industry, Hiring Requirements and Employment of Disadvantaged Groups* (New York: New York University School of

38   Youth Employment in American Industry

Commerce, 1970); Paul E. Barton, "Youth Employment and Career Entry," in Seymour L. Wolfbein, ed., *Labor Market Information for Youths* (Philadelphia: Temple University Press, 1975), pp. 89-90.

9. Robison, p. 9.
10. Robert Taggart, *A Fisherman's Guide: An Assessment of Training and Remediation Strategies* (Kalamazoo, Mich.: W. E. UpJohn Institute for Employment Research, 1981), pp. 117-18, 122.
11. Ibid., p. 119.
12. Youth Programs, pp. 13-16.
13. Greenleigh Associates, *Job Opportunities in the Business Sector Program* (New York: Greenleigh 1970). An age breakdown of survey's sample respondents showed, however, that less than half of the participants were 25 and under.
14. National Commission for Manpower Policy, "Corporate Hiring Practices," in *From School to Work: Improving the Transition* (Washington, D.C.: National Commission for Manpower Policy, 1976), p. 39.
15. Chamber of Commerce of the United States, *A Survey of Federal Employment and Training Programs* (Washington, D.C.: Chamber of Commerce of the United States, September 1978). This study, however, was not targeted specifically to young CETA trainees.
16. Allen R. Janger, *Employing the Disadvantaged: A Company Perspective* (New York: Conference Board, 1972), p. 60.

6
Occupations and Hiring Patterns of Minority Youths

The jobless problem is especially acute among black and other minority youths, whose unemployment rates are usually two to three times higher than those of white youths. Several writers have termed black youths an "endangered species" because of the escalating numbers of jobless youths who have been frustrated in their attempts to find work.[1] In fact, it is the persistent and increasing decline in the labor force participation of nonwhite youths that constitutes the center of the youth joblessness problem.[2] Despite the fact that black youths have increased their educational attainment at a faster rate than white youths, this increase has not netted higher employment rates. This fact runs counter to the human capital theory that black subgroups show lesser employment potential.[3] Hence, the issue of youth joblessness largely becomes "one of explaining reduced employment of minority youth."[4]

Experts across many disciplines have attempted to explain high unemployment among black and other nonwhite youths. Where does the truth lie with respect to minority youth unemployment? Is it race alone that accounts for their impoverished position in the labor market? Is it solely class? That is, do white youths from low-income and disadvantaged backgrounds have the same experiences? Or is it a combination of the two? Robert Hill, former director of the National Urban League Research Department, argued that most of the causes of minority youth joblessness can be attributed, in varying degrees, to discrimination:

> Most of the . . . "causes" (e.g. educational attainment and movement of industries from central cities and periodic recessions) of minority youth joblessness are themselves to varying degrees determined by discrimination. For example, the fact that minority youth disproportionately reside in central cities is in part due to discriminatory housing patterns in suburban areas. . . . And, finally, the discriminatory barriers to quality education for minority youth have been conclusively and repeatedly documented.[5]

Other research also supports the thesis that race has a significant negative effect on a youth's employment status even after taking education, location, age, and family background into account.[6] For example, Osterman's analysis controlled for family income of black and white youths and found that race is the key to explaining black youth unemployment. Racial discrimination accounted for "roughly 50% of the unemployment differential" between black and white youths.[7]

Further, in a series of informal dialogues between employers and educators sponsored by the Vice-President's Task Force on Youth Employment, a major finding was that the racial discrimination continues to influence the hiring of minority youths. In addition, a pervasive attitude among large and small employers was that "social commitment" to hiring more minority youths conflicted with internal productivity goals. In other words, many employers viewed the recruitment of minorities as a social choice that could erode productivity! Employers also believed that considerable company follow-through or "parenting" inflated the cost of the social choice to hire more minority youths.[8]

In this chapter, we describe the occupational representation and hiring patterns for minority youths. We also profile the companies that have special jobs programs for minority youths.

Occupational Representation of Minority Youths

In what occupations are minority youths, aged 16-24, typically located in American businesses? Employers were asked to identify the *one* position in which minority youths employed by their companies tended to be *most* concentrated. Figure 6.1 depicts the occupational representation of minority youths based on the number of firms (473) that responded to the question.

Not surprisingly, the largest percentage of minority youths, aged 16-24, were concentrated in service (28%) and laborer (19%) jobs. These youths were least likely to occupy professional/mangerial/technical (4%) and crafts (2%) positions. Below we analyze the typical positions of minority youths by employer characteristics of business type and business size. Specifically, we sought to discover whether type and size of business were related to the occupations that minority youths typically occupy in terms of the white-collar/blue-collar classification.[9]

FIGURE 6.1
POSITIONS MINORITY YOUTHS TYPICALLY OCCUPY

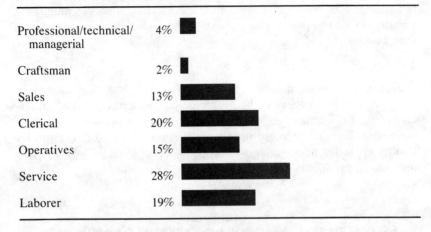

Professional/technical/ managerial	4%	
Craftsman	2%	
Sales	13%	
Clerical	20%	
Operatives	15%	
Service	28%	
Laborer	19%	

Note: Percentages may not add to 100 due to rounding.

TABLE 6.1
ESTIMATED PERCENTAGE OF JOB TYPES HELD BY MINORITY YOUTHS, BY TYPE OF BUSINESS

Job Type	Manufacturing	Trade	Finance	Service	Other[a]
White Collar	10	49	89	22	13
Blue Collar	90	51	11	74	87
Total	100	100	100	100	100
Sample Size	(79)	(126)	(45)	(136)	(30)

a. Other businesses include mining, agriculture, construction, and transportation.
Note: Percentages may not add to 100 due to rounding.

Business Type

Occupations that minority youths occupy are related to the type of firm. Minority youths usually hold blue-collar occupations in nine out of 10 manufacturing (90%) and "other" (87%) businesses. They are also concentrated in blue-collar jobs in three-fourths of the service firms (74%). In finance businesses, however, minority youths occupy white-collar jobs in nine out of 10 (89%) of these firms. The typical occupations for minority youths in trade establishments, though, are equally divided between white-collar (49%) and blue-collar (51%) jobs (see Table 6.1).

Business Size

Size of business, however, is not related to the occupations of minority youths. As revealed in Table 6.2, about three-fifths of minority youths hold blue-collar jobs in the majority of firms regardless of size. Sixty-one (61) percent of the small firms reported that minority youths typically occupy blue-collar jobs, compared to 64% for medium-sized establishments and 66% for large firms.

TABLE 6.2
ESTIMATED PERCENTAGE OF JOB TYPES HELD BY MINORITY YOUTHS, BY SIZE OF BUSINESS

	Size		
Job Type	Small (1-99)	Medium (100-249)	Large (250 & over)
White Collar	39	37	34
Blue Collar	61	64	66
Total	100	100	100
Sample Size	(71)	(211)	(134)

Note: Percentages may not add to 100 due to rounding.

Hiring Patterns for All Minority Youths

What were the hiring patterns for minority youths over the past year among the national sample of businesses? Employers were asked whether their company hired "many more," "about the same," or "fewer or none" minority youths, aged 16-24, over the past 12 months compared to the previous year. For greater specificity in describing the hiring patterns for minority youths, minorities were broken into the following five subgroups: American Indian or Alaskan native; Asian or

Pacific islander; black, not of Hispanic origin; Hispanic; and other racial minorities.

Figure 6.2 shows that two-thirds of the firms hired "fewer or none" American Indians or Alaskan natives, aged 16-24, compared to the previous year. A similar majority pattern held for hiring of Asian or Pacific islander youths (55%) as well as for "other" racial minority youths (64%). For Hispanic youths, aged 16-24, about one-third of the

FIGURE 6.2
HIRING PATTERNS FOR MINORITY YOUTHS COMPARED TO THE PREVIOUS YEAR AS REPORTED BY ALL BUSINESSES

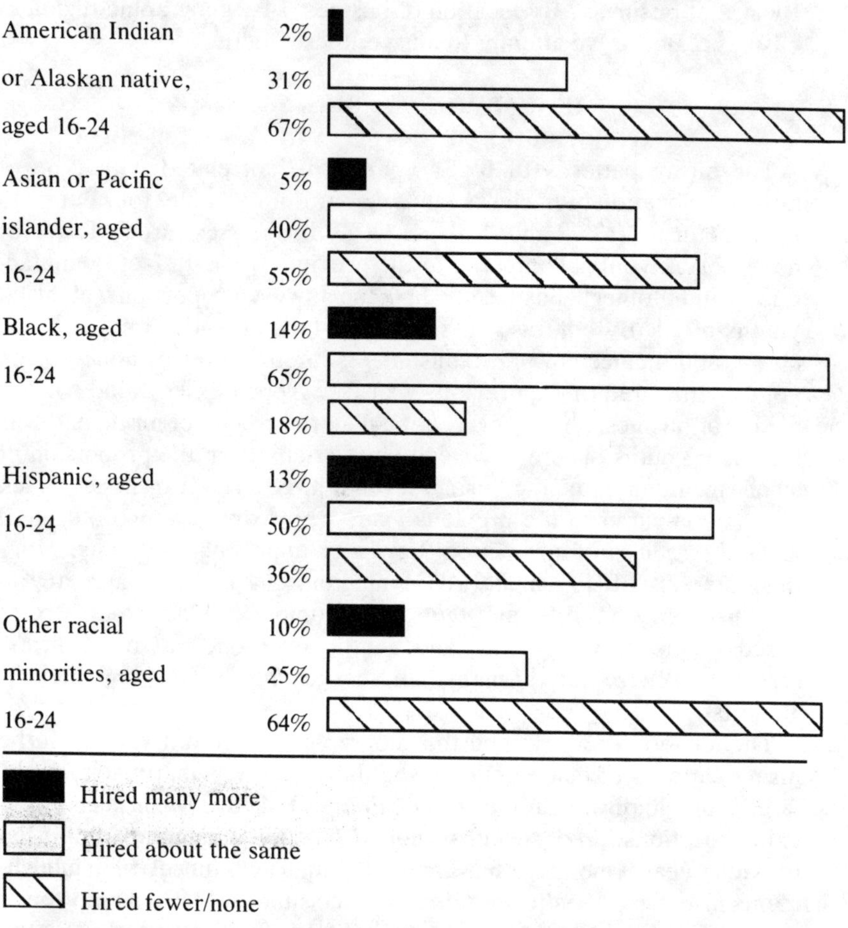

American Indian	2%
or Alaskan native,	31%
aged 16-24	67%
Asian or Pacific	5%
islander, aged	40%
16-24	55%
Black, aged	14%
16-24	65%
	18%
Hispanic, aged	13%
16-24	50%
	36%
Other racial	10%
minorities, aged	25%
16-24	64%

Hired many more
Hired about the same
Hired fewer/none

establishments (36%) reported hiring "fewer or none," while half (50%) hired "about the same" number of Hispanic youths during the current year compared to the previous year. For black youths, aged 16-24, about one-fifth (18%) of the businesses surveyed hired "fewer or none" compared to the previous year, while two-thirds (65%) hired "about the same" number of black youths. It is important to underscore the point that only a small minority of the firms surveyed hired "many more" minority youths of any subgroup.

In the following sections, we profile the hiring patterns of black and Hispanic youths by employer characteristics of business type, size, location, and geographic region. Thus, the significant questions are: Do hiring patterns for black and Hispanic youths vary by type of business? By size of business? By location of business? By geographic region of business? Below we attempt to answer these queries.

Hiring Patterns for Black Youths

The hiring patterns of black youths are correlated with type of business, location of business, and region. For example, four out of 10 manufacturing (37%) and "other" (40%) businesses hired "fewer or none" black youths compared to the previous year. In fact, manufacturing and "other" businesses had the lowest proportions of black youths hired. By contrast, less than one-fifth of trade (14%), service (14%), and finance (16%) establishments hired "fewer or none" black youths compared to the previous year (see Appendix D, Table A).

Size of business, however, is not a major correlate of hiring patterns for black youths. There is virtually no variability in the proportion of small, medium, and large businesses that hired "fewer or none" black youths compared to the previous year. Approximately two out of 10 firms, regardless of size, hired "fewer or none" black youths. More than six out of 10 small (61%), medium (64%), and large (69%) establishments hired "about the same" number of black youths compared to the previous year; and a little over one out of 10 firms, regardless of size, hired "many more" black youths (see Appendix D, Table B).

The location of a firm and the geographic region did vary with the hiring patterns of black youths. The data indicated that black youths fared worst in rural/exurb locations. Four out of 10 (39%) firms in rural/exurb locations hired "fewer or none" black youths compared to the previous year. One the other hand, less than two out of 10 establishments in central cities/towns (19%) and the suburbs (15%) hired "fewer or none" black youths during the current year compared to the previous year (see Appendix D, Table C). When hiring patterns were analyzed by geographic region, black youths fared best in the South. Only five percent of businesses in the south hired "fewer or none" black youths compared to the previous year. In the Northeast, one-third of the firms (33%) hired "fewer or none" black youths compared to about thee out of 10 (28%) in the North-Central region and one-fourth (23%) of the firms in the West (see Appendix D, Table D).

Hiring Patterns for Hispanic Youths

The hiring patterns of Hispanic youths also vary, in some instances, by employer characteristics. When broken down by type of business, manufacturing and "other" businesses hired the lowest proportions of Hispanic youths of all establishments as in the case of black youths. Half of the manufacturing firms (51%) and four out of 10 "other" businesses (42%) hired "fewer or none" Hispanic youths compared to the previous year. By comparison, nearly three out of 10 trade (28%), finance (26%), and service (30%) firms hired "fewer or none" Hispanic youths compared to the previous year (see Appendix D, Table E).

Size of business did not vary appreciably with hiring patterns for Hispanic youths—as was the case for black youths. There were no large substantive differences in the proportion of small, medium, and large businesses that hired "fewer or none" Hispanic youths compared to the previous year. Three out of 10 small (29%) and large (32%) firms, and about four out of 10 medium-sized firms (38%) hired "fewer or none" Hispanic youths compared to the previous year. Approximately half of the establishments of all sizes hired "about the same" number of Hispanic youths, while less than two out of 10 firms, regardless of size, hired "fewer or none" Hispanic youths compared to the previous year (see Appendix D, Table F).

The location and geographic region of the firms, however, did vary with the hiring patterns for Hispanic youths. The data indicated that Hispanic youths, similar to black youths, fared worst in rural/exurb locations. Half (53%) of the establishments in rural/exurb locations hired "fewer or none" Hispanic youths compared to the previous year. By contrast, about one-third of the firms located in central cities/towns (32%) and suburbs (35%) hired "fewer or none" Hispanic youths compared to the previous year (see Appendix D, Table G). When hiring patterns were analyzed by geographic region, Hispanic youths fared best in the western region. Only one out of 10 of the firms (10%) in the West hired "fewer or none" Hispanic youths compared to the previous year. In the South, one-third (33%) of the establishments hired "fewer or none" Hispanic youths compared to the previous year. In the Northeast, four out of 10 (42%) of the businesses hired "fewer or none" Hispanic youths, compared to about half in the North-Central (46%) and southern (53%) regions (see Appendix D, Table H).

Special Jobs Programs for Minority Youths

Minority youths need special career and vocational attention due to the prevailing effects of racial discrimination in the marketplace, the lack of quality education, as well as other factors. A study by the Conference Board provides some supportive evidence of private industry's recognition of the need to pay "special attention to raising the aspirations or broadening career choices for minorities." While a slightly higher proportion of the establishments surveyed made this assertion about women, "paying special attention" took two forms: (1) special efforts to bring more young minority members and women into the reach of company programs, and (2) use of special measures to orient minority and women students to opportunities in careers likely to be unfamiliar or regarded as unattainable.[10]

Other research has also shown that some companies have developed special recruitment and training programs for minorities. Although these programs are not usually targeted on youth, young people do participate in them.[11] In the following section, we profile the companies in our survey that reported having participated in special jobs programs for minority youths.

Companies with Special Jobs Programs for Minority Youths

Only 27 firms reported having *current* jobs training programs targeted for minority youths. In addition, only 19 firms reported having had a targeted jobs programs for minority youths in the past. Based on these responses, the overwhelming majority (over 90%) of businesses surveyed *never* had a jobs programs targeted to minority youths.

Companies with current jobs programs for minority youths were asked the following question: "Approximately how many minority youths, aged 16-24, participated in your jobs training program during the latest complete year of operation?" The employers' responses ranged from one to three minority participants. Most of the firms reported that the minority youth job programs were company funded. Approximately half of the employers with current jobs programs for minority youths considered the programs to be "successful" in achieving its goals, while the other half considered the programs to be "somewhat successful." The employers were also asked to respond to the following question: "What do you expect your company's level of participation in its jobs program for minority youth will be over the next two years?" Eleven responded that the participation rate would "remain the same," seven projected an "increase" in participation, one expected a "decrease," and five answered "don't know."

Finally, the firms were asked to make additional comments about the jobs programs for minority youths. Below are some of the employers' responses:

- We participated with other employers and a nonprofit organization entitled "Inroads," for the increased utilization of minorities. In professional positions through education, counseling, and summer training on-the-job work experience. "Inroads" operates in Chicago, St. Louis, Charlestown, West Virginia.

- In our small rural community we were involved with the local high school on providing OJT positions. We also employ students as summer employees.

- Our help is seasonal—service technicians work on appliances, air conditioners, furnaces etc. We haven't hired anyone full time for five years.

- Since we are in the health care field, we are very careful in the selection of new employees. Also we have a very intensive orientation program which has proven to reduce turnover.

Special jobs programs for minority youths, as the figures show are, indeed, rare among this national sample. Apparently, there is a general unwillingness in the private sector to target special programs for the employment of minority youths who historically have had higher unemployment rates than white youths.

Summary of Findings

Occupational Representation of Minority Youth

- Two-thirds (67%) of all businesses surveyed indicated that minority youths are most concentrated in three occupations: service (28%), clerical (20%), and laborers (19%). Less than one-tenth (6%) of the firms indicated that minority youths were most concentrated in craft (2%) and professional/managerial/technical (4%) positions.
- Three-fourths or more of the businesses in manufacturing (90%), service (74%), and "other" (87%) industries said that minority youth held blue-collar jobs, compared to only half (51%) of the trade and one-tenth (11%) of the finance establishments.
- Regardless of their size, six out of 10 small (61%), medium-sized

(64%), and large (66%) businesses said that their minority youth employees were most concentrated in blue-collar jobs.

Hiring Patterns of Minority Youths

- Eight out of 10 (79%) firms surveyed reported hiring about the same (65%) or more (14%) black youths than they did the previous year, while only two out of 10 (18%) hired fewer black youths.
- Six out of 10 (63%) of the businesses surveyed said they hired about the same (50%) or more (13%) Hispanic youths than they did the previous year, while almost four out of 10 (36%) said that they hired fewer Hispanic youths.
- Trade, finance, and service businesses hire minority youth to a greater extent than manufacturing and "other" businesses. Eight out of 10 trade (86%), finance (85%), and service (86%) firms hired about the same or more black youths than they did the previous year, compared to six out of 10 manufacturing (63%) and "other" (60%) establishments. Similarly, about seven out of 10 trade (72%), finance (74%), and service (71%) firms hired about the same or more Hispanic youths, compared to five out of 10 manufacturing (49%) and "other" (57%) businesses.
- Hiring patterns of minority youths do not vary by size of business. About eight out of 10 small (76%), medium-sized (79%), and large (81%) businesses hired about the same or more black youths than they did the previous year. Seven out of 10 small (71%) and large (69%) businesses hired about the same or more Hispanic youths than they did the previous year, compared to six out of 10 medium-sized (62%) firms.
- Minority youths are more likely to be hired by firms in central cities and suburbs than by those in rural/exurban areas. Eight out of 10 businesses in central cities (82%) and the suburbs (85%) hired about the same or more black youths than they did the previous year, compared to six out of 10 (61%) businesses in rural or exurban areas. Similarly, two-thirds of the firms in central cities (68%) and the suburbs (65%) hired about the same or more Hispanic youths, compared to only half (47%) of the firms in rural/exurban areas.
- Southern firms report hiring more black youths recently than firms outside the South. Almost all (95%) of the firms in the South said they hired more or about the same number of minority youths than in the previous year, compared to about seven out of 10 businesses in the West (77%), Northeast (68%), and North-Central (72%) regions.
- Firms in the West report hiring more Hispanic youths recently than businesses in other regions. Nine out of 10 (90%) businesses in the West hired about the same or more Hispanic youths than in the previous year, compared to about six out of 10 businesses in the South (66%), Northeast (58%), and North-Central (54%) regions.

• Less than 1% (or 27) of the 535 businesses surveyed currently have special jobs programs targeted to minority youths.

Notes

1. Francis Ward wrote that black youths are becoming an "endangered species," in *First World Magazine* (Jan./Feb. 1977), cf. "Editorial," *Urban League Review* III (Winter, 1977). See also James D. McGhee, "The Black Teenager: An Endangered Species," in National Urban League, *State of Black America, 1982* (New York: National Urban League, January 1982), pp. 171-96.
2. Richard B. Freeman, "Why Is There a Youth Labor Market Problem?" in *Youth Employment and Public Policy,* Bernard E. Anderson and Isabel Sawhill, eds. (Englewood Cliffs, N.J.: Prentice Hall, 1980), p. 9.
3. Denys Vaughn-Cooke, "Causes of Teenage and Youth Unemployment," unpublished paper (Washington, D.C.: Urban Institute, June 1980).
4. Ibid., p. 9.
5. Robert B. Hill, "Discrimination and Minority Youth Unemployment," in the Vice-President's Task Force on Youth Employment, *A Review of Youth Employment Programs and Policies* (Washington, D.C., 1980).
6. U.S. Department of Labor, *The Nature of the Youth Employment Problem: A Review Paper,* Technical Analysis Paper no. 69 (Washington, D.C., March 1980).
7. Paul Osterman, "The Employment Problems of Black Youth: A Review of the Evidence and Some Policy Suggestions," in *Expanding Employment Opportunities for Disadvantaged Youth: Sponsored Research* (Washington, D.C.: National Commission for Employment Policy, 1979), pp. 93, 94, 129.
8. Erik P. Butler and James Darr, *Research on Youth Employment and Employability Development: Educator and Employer Perspectives* (Waltham, Mass.: Brandeis University Press, May 1980), pp. 27-28.
9. Blue-collar occupations were defined as craftsmen, operatives, service, and laborers. White-collar occupations were defined as professional/technical/managerial, sales, and clerical.
10. Seymour Lusterman and Harriet Gorlin, *Educating Students for Work: Some Business Roles* (New York: Conference Board, 1980), p. 11.
11. Butler and Darr, p. 28.

7

Participation in Government Jobs Programs

Over the past two decades, the federal government instituted a broad range of employment and training programs in the public and private sectors for unemployed and underemployed adults and youth. These programs tend to fall into three categories: employability development for all age groups, work experience and training programs for youth, and tax credits for hiring the structurally unemployed. We will describe each of these three types of government programs.

Description of Key Jobs Programs

Employability Development Programs

Employability development programs are designed to: (1) provide skill training, basic education, counseling, vocational training, and work experience in classroom settings as well as on the job; (2) create jobs through public service and subsidized private-sector employment, and (3) offer supportive services, such as child care, transportation, medical, housing, or other assistance needed to enhance employability.

The first comprehensive government jobs program was the Manpower Development and Training Act (MDTA) of 1962, which was designed originally to provide institutional retraining for adult workers who had been displaced by technological advances or had not recovered from the severe 1960-61 recession. However, as a result of accelerated economic growth and passage of the "War on Poverty's" Economic Opportunity Act of 1964, racially and economically disadvantaged groups became the primary MDTA target population. Some of the employability development programs (not targeted to youth) instituted during the 1960s were: institutional training, on-the-job training (OJT), vocational rehabilitation, the Public Employment Program (PEP), the Work Incentive Program (WIN), the Concentrated Employment Program (CEP), and Operation Mainstream. The National Alliance of Businessman's JOBS Program, which provided on-the-job training for the disadvantaged, was the major private sector initiative during the sixties.

However, with the advent of the Nixon administration in 1969, many of the antipoverty programs were totally dismantled, had their funds sharply reduced or frozen, or were radically transformed. For example, as a result of President Nixon's "New Federalism" efforts to decentralize the administration of government social programs to states and localities, many of the categorical programs of the sixties were combined into broad "revenue-sharing" block grants. Examples of the block grants instituted by the Nixon administration were the Community Development Block Grant to replace Model Cities and the Comprehensive Employment and Training Act (CETA) to replace the MDTA and Title XX in social services.

The CETA programs consisted of classroom training, on-the-job training, public service employment, work experience, the Job Corps, and the Summer Youth Program. Since CETA funds were distributed by formula to many suburban localities with relatively low levels of unemployment, minorities and other economically disadvantaged groups were less adequately represented in the decentralized CETA program than they were in the categorical MDTA programs. However, by 1977, the Carter administration succeeded in obtaining congressional legislation to target the CETA jobs programs more effectively to the economically disadvantaged.

Youth Programs

The major programs that were targeted to youth during the 1960s were: the Jobs Corps, the Neighborhood Youth Corps (which included in-school, out-of-school, and summer programs), and the Apprenticeship Outreach Program to increase the participation of minority youth in the skilled trades. Sizable numbers of youths were also served by the MDTA's classroom training and on-the-job training programs. During the sixties and seventies the National Urban League and its affiliates were major conduits for providing vital employment and training services to minority youth in both the private and public sectors through its apprenticeship outreach and on-the-job training programs that were funded by the U.S. Department of Labor.

However, the most comprehensive jobs programs for youth were instituted by the Carter administration through the Youth Employment and Demonstration Project Act (YEDP) of 1977. The YEDP established the following programs:

• The Youth Employment and Training Program (YETP), which was designed to enhance the job prospects and career preparation of low-income youth through a broad range of training and supportive

services, such as apprenticeships, high school equivalency or GED
certification, job sampling, transportation subsidies, and special focus on in-school youth.
• The Job Corps, provided basic education, vocational training, and
work experience to disadvantaged youth in residential settings.
• Summer Youth Employment Program, which provided vocational
counseling, work experience, on-the-job training, career preparation,
and remedial education to youths from all economic backgrounds.
• Young Adult Conservation Corps, which provided work experience
to youth from all socioeconomic backgrounds through work on
conservation and other projects on federal and nonfederal lands and
waters.
• The Youth Community Conservation and Improvement Projects,
which developed the vocational preparation of out-of-school, jobless
youth through well-supervised work of community benefit that had
the possibility of receiving academic credit for work experience
through cooperative vocational education.
• The Youth Incentive Entitlement Pilot Projects, which was an experi-
mental program to provide subsidized jobs in the private sector at
minimum and subminimum wages to unemployed school dropouts if
and only if they returned to complete high school or pursue high
school equivalency. The level of wage subsidies varied from 50% to
100% of the minimum wage in 17 communities.

Subminimum Wage Youth Certificates

A less-publicized government program designed to increase employment opportunities for young people is the Subminimum Wage Youth
Certificate Program. This program has its antecedents in the original
Fair Labor Standard Act (FLSA) of 1935, which established the federal
minimum wage and overtime provisions. In its early years, the FLSA
permitted subminimum wages to learners, apprentices, trainees, and
messengers. In 1961, a provision was instituted to permit the payment
of wages at 85% of the federal minimum wage to full-time students in
the public and private sectors. Employers must obtain a special exemp-
tion certificate from the U.S. Labor Department in order to hire no
more than six full-time students at any one establishment.

Large numbers of young people are hired each year through this
certificate program. For example, in fiscal year (FY) 1976, the Labor
Department issued 1,191 subminimum wage certificates to institutions
of higher education for 459,000 full-time students, and 19,919 certificates were issued to retail or service establishments for 153,000 full-
time students. Interestingly, studies have revealed relatively low utilization by private employers of their approved certificates. However,

there have been few systematic national surveys of employers to determine the actual extent of knowledge about and utilization of the subminimum wage certificates.

Tax Credit Jobs Programs

An approach that is being used increasingly as an incentive to the private sector to hire disadvantaged persons are tax credits. The first such tax expenditure jobs program was the Work Incentive Tax Credit enacted as part of the WIN II program in the Revenue Act of 1971. The WIN tax credit was designed to help AFDC recipients registered in the Work Incentive Program (WIN) to obtain employment in the private sector by providing tax credits up to 50% of the first-year wages of each eligible employee, up to 25% of the second-year wages, and up to 50% reimbursement for on-the-job training costs. Unused WIN tax credits may be carried backward or forward against the employer's tax liability for other years. A fast tax write-off is also permitted for expenditures on facilities used for on-the-job training of employees or as day care centers for their children. Between FY 1973 and FY 1974 the number of placements made in jobs involving WIN tax credits rose from 25,000 to 40,000.

The second major tax credit designed to induce jobs in the private sector was the New Jobs Tax Credit (NJTC) enacted in 1977. The NJTC, which was not targeted to groups in the workforce, was designed to provide special tax breaks for firms based on the number of *new* jobs that they created. However, because of its complexity and unworkability, it was quickly replaced by the Targeted Jobs Tax Credit (TJTC) under the Revenue Act of 1978. The TJTC also replaced the WIN Tax Credit and the Vocational Rehabilitation Tax Credit, which expired on December 31, 1978.

As one of the Carter administration's urban policy proposals, the Targeted Jobs Tax Credit was limited originally to hires of economically disadvantaged youth, aged 18-24, and to students in cooperative education programs regardless of economic background. But its coverage was broadened significantly under its reauthorization as part of the Economic Recovery Tax Act of 1981. Employers can now obtain Targeted Jobs Tax Credits if they hire persons from one of the following seven categories:

1. Supplemental Security Income (SSI) recipients.
2. Handicapped individuals referred by U.S. vocational rehabilitation agencies or by the Veterans Administration.
3. Economically disadvantaged Vietnam-era veterans under 35 years old.

4. Economically disadvantaged youth 18-24 years old.
5. Economically disadvantaged ex-convicts.
6. WIN and other welfare recipients.
7. Economically disadvantaged youth 16-19 years old participating in an approved cooperative education program.

The Targeted Jobs Tax Credit allows employers to claim a tax credit of 50% of the first year wages (up to $6,000) and 25% of the second year wages (up to $6,000). However, because an employer's normal deductions for wages must be reduced by the amount of the tax credit claimed, net TJTC savings can range from $900 per hire for an employer in the 70% tax bracket to $2,580 for one in the 14% bracket for each eligible employee paid $6,000 for the first year of employment. The law also permits employers to apply for a tax credit on a retroactive basis, that is, after an employee in one of the seven eligible categories had already been hired.

In fact, a study of the original TJTC revealed that three-fourths of the certificates obtained during the summer of 1981 were retroactive. During the first two and a half years (i.e., between second quarters 1979 and 1981), TJTC provided wage subsidies for about 605,000 target group workers. Disadvantaged youth accounted for 40% of those hires, cooperative education students for 45%, and the other target groups comprised the remaining 15%. Clearly, the TJTC appears to be an important medium for increasing employment opportunities for disadvantaged youth in the private sector.

Knowledge and Use of Jobs Programs

Employability Development

Employers were asked about their knowledge of and participation in two employability development programs for workers of all ages: CETA on-the-job training and CETA job upgrading and training. While nine-tenths (87%) of the employers had heard about the OJT program, only one-fourth (24%) had actually participated in it. On the other hand, although 57% of the employers knew about the job upgrading and retraining program, only 10% had participated in it (see Table 7.1).

Youth Jobs Programs

Employers were less knowledgeable about specific jobs programs for youth than they were about employability development programs in general. For example, only one-fourth (22%) were familiar with the SPEDY Summer Youth Program for disadvantaged youth and only 4% had participated in it. Similarly, although 37% had heard about the

TABLE 7.1
**KNOWLEDGE AND UTILIZATION OF EMPLOYABILITY
DEVELOPMENT PROGRAMS**

	(% "Yes")	
Employability Development	Heard of	Used
1. CETA On-the Job Training (OJT) Program	87%	24%
2. CETA Job Upgrading and Retraining Programs	57%	10%

subminimum wage certificate program for students, only 3% of them had used those youth certificates. However, two-thirds (66%) of the employers had heard about the overall CETA youth employment and training programs, while 13% had participated in them (see Table 7.2).

Jobs Tax Credits

But jobs tax credit programs had the greatest popularity among private employers. Eight out of 10 (79%) employers were familiar with the Work Incentive (WIN) tax credits for hiring welfare recipients, and 22% of them used those credits. Similarly, while 73% of the employers had heard about the Target Jobs Tax Credit (TJTC) program, fully one-third (34%) of them had used the TJTC (see Table 7.3).

TABLE 7.2
KNOWLEDGE AND UTILIZATION OF YOUTH JOBS PROGRAMS

	(% "Yes")	
Youth Jobs Programs	Heard of	Used
1. CETA Youth Employment & Training Programs	66%	13%
2. Summer Youth Program	22%	4%
3. Subminimum Wage Youth Certificate	37%	3%

Thus, the three government jobs programs with the highest participation among private employers were the Targeted Jobs Tax Credits (34%), the CETA OJT program (24%), and the WIN tax credits (22%). What kinds of firms participated in these programs? Were they more likely to be service, manufacturing, or trade? Were they more likely to

TABLE 7.3
KNOWLEDGE AND UTILIZATION OF JOBS TAX CREDITS

	(% "Yes")	
Jobs Tax Credits Programs	Heard of	Used
1. Work Incentive (WIN) Tax Credit	79%	22%
2. Targeted Jobs Tax Credits (TJTC)	73%	34%

be small or large businesses? Were they more likely to be located in the suburbs or central cities? We shall attempt to obtain answers to some of these questions by examining the patterns of usage of these three programs by various characteristics of businesses.

Patterns of Usage of Key Jobs Programs

Targeted Jobs Tax Credits (TJTC)

Employers in the trade industry had the highest (63%) usage of Targeted Jobs Tax Credits, while those in services had the lowest (23%) usage. And employers in manufacturing (39%) and finance (39%) had intermediate levels of usage of the TJTC.

The usage of the TJTC did vary markedly by size of business, with small businesses having the highest levels. While half (47%) of the firms with less than 100 employees used the TJTC, only two-fifths of the firms with 100-249 employees (38%) and with 250 or more employees (40%) used the Targeted Jobs Tax Credits.

Suburban businesses had the highest usage of the TJTC, while rural firms had the lowest usage. About half (45%) of the employers in the suburbs used the TJTC, compared to only 39% of the firms in central cities and to only 32% of the businesses in rural areas.

Utilization of the TJTC was directly related to the proportion of young people employed. While 57% of the firms with a high proportion (10% or more) of teenagers employed used the TJTC, only 22% of those with a low proportion (0-1%) of teenagers used the TJTC. Similarly, half (46%) of the companies with a high proportion (25% and over) of young adults employed used the TJTC, compared to only 31% of those with a low proportion (under 15%) of young adults (see Table 7.4).

TABLE 7.4
USE OF TARGETED JOBS TAX CREDITS, BY EMPLOYER
CHARACTERISTICS
(PERCENT THAT USED TJTC)

A. Type of Business

(82)[a] Manufacturing	(129)[a] Trade	(41)[a] Finance	(123)[a] Service	(33)[a] Other[b]
39%	63%	39%	23%	24%

B. Size of Business

(68) Under 100 Employees	(205) 100-249	(126) 250 and over
47%	38%	40%

C. Location of Business

(230) Central City	(137) Suburbs	(81) Rural
39%	45%	32%

D. Proportion of Teenagers Employed

(132) Low (0-1%)	(154) Moderate (2-9%)	(170) High (10% and over)
22%	37%	57%

E. Proportion of Young Adults Employed

(139) Low (0-14%)	(125) Moderate (15-24%)	(192) High (25% and over)
31%	40%	46%

a. Numbers in parentheses refer to sample sizes in each category.
b. "Other" includes agriculture, mining, construction, and transportation.

Work Incentive (WIN) Tax Credits

The utilization of WIN tax credits varied little by type of business. The usage of these tax credits in the service industry (31%) was only somewhat higher than the usage in manufacturing (27%), trade (25%), and finance (25%). Similarly, the usage of WIN tax credits by companies with 250 or more employees (31%) was only slightly higher than the usage by firms with less than 100 (25%) and between 100 and 249 (23%) employees.

Likewise, the utilization of WIN tax credits did not vary by location of business. One-fourth of the companies used these credits, regardless of whether or not they were in central cities (25%), the suburbs (26%), or rural (24%) areas.

On the other hand, the utilization of WIN tax credits was directly related to the proportion of youth employed. While almost one-third (31%) of the companies with a high proportion of teenage employees used the WIN tax credits, twice as many (32%) of the firms with a high proportion of young adult employees used them (see Table 7.5).

CETA On-the-Job Training

Participation in the CETA on-the-job training program varied markedly by type of business. Two-fifths (42%) of the companies in the service sector participated in the OJT program, compared to only one-fourth (24%) of the firms in manufacturing and one-fifth in trade (21%) and finance (22%). Interestingly, participation in the OJT program had a curvilinear relationship with size of business. Thus, medium-sized firms (100-249 employees) had the lowest participation (24%) in the OJT program, while the small (28%) and large (34%) businesses had the highest levels of participation.

However, there was little difference in participation in the OJT program by location of business. While three-tenths of the firms in central cities (29%) and rural areas (29%) used OJT, about one-fourth (24%) of the firms in the suburbs also participated.

OJT participation was lowest among companies with low levels of youth employees. For example, the proportion of companies in OJT was twice as great among those with moderate (2-9%) proportions of teenage employees than among those with low proportions (0-1%) of teenage employees. At the same time, one-fourth (26%) of the firms with high proportions (10% or more) of teenage employees participated in the OJT program.

However, participation in OJT did not vary markedly by the proportion of young adults employed. The proportion of firms participating in OJT was only slightly lower among those with low levels of young adult employees (26%) than among companies with moderate (27%) or high (29%) proportions of young adult employees (see Table 7.6).

Relationships between Programs

Utilization of the Targeted Jobs Tax Credits (TJTC) was strongly correlated with use of the WIN tax credits. While almost half (44%) of the firms that used the UJTC also used the WIN credits, only 13% of

TABLE 7.5
USE OF WORK INCENTIVE TAX CREDITS, BY EMPLOYER CHARACTERISTICS
(PERCENT THAT USED WIN TAX CREDITS)

A. Type of Business

(81)[a] Manufacturing	(114)[a] Trade	(40)[a] Finance	(128)[a] Service	(34)[a] Other[b]
27%	25%	25%	31%	9%

B. Size of Business

(67) Under 100 Employees	(202) 100-249	(128) 250 & over
25%	23%	31%

C. Location of Business

(230) Central City	(134) Suburbs	(82) Rural
25%	26%	24%

D. Proportion of Teenagers Employed

(133) Low (0-1%)	(152) Moderate (2-9%)	(169) High (10% and over)
19%	25%	31%

E. Proportion of Young Adults Employed

(138) Low (0-14%)	(124) Moderate (15-24%)	(192) High (25% & over)
15%	27%	32%

a. Numbers in parentheses refer to a sample sizes in each category.
b. "Other" includes agriculture, mining, construction, and transportation.

TABLE 7.6
USE OF CETA ON-THE-JOB TRAINING PROGRAM, BY EMPLOYER
CHARACTERISTICS
(PERCENT THAT USED CETA-OJT PROGRAM)

A. Type of Business

(81) [a] Manufacturing	(118) [a] Trade	(41) [a] Finance	(137) [a] Service	(35) [a] Other [b]
24%	21%	22%	42%	11%

A. Size of Business

(71) Under 100 Employees	(204) 100-249	(137) 250 and over
28%	24%	34%

C. Location of Business

(237) Central City	(141) Suburbs	(85) Rural
29%	26%	29%

D. Proportion of Teenagers Employed

(136) Low (0-1%)	(160) Moderate (2-9%)	(176) High (10% and Over)
20%	36%	26%

E. Proportion of Young Adults Employed

(144) Low (0-14%)	(128) Moderate (15-24%)	(200) High (25% and Over)
26%	27%	29%

a. Numbers in parentheses refer to sample sizes in each category.
b. "Other" includes agriculture, mining, construction, and transportation.

the firms that did not use TJTC used the WIN tax credits (see Table 7.7).

TABLE 7.7
**USE OF THE WORK INCENTIVE PROGRAM (WIN), BY USE OF THE
TARGETED JOBS TAX CREDIT (1978)
(PERCENTAGE DISTRIBUTION)**

	Use of Tax Credit	
Use of WIN	Yes	No
Yes	44	13
No	57	87
Total	100	100
Sample Size	(170)	(267)

Note: Percentages may not add to 100 due to rounding.

TJTC utilization was also related to participation in the OJT program, although not as strong as the correlation with use of WIN tax credits. While one-fourth (23%) of the firms that did not use the TJTC participated in OJT, one-third (31%) of the companies that used the TJTC also participated in the CETA OJT program (see Table 7.8).

TABLE 7.8
**USE OF THE CETA-OJT TRAINING SUBSIDY, BY USE OF THE
TARGETED JOBS TAX CREDIT, 1978
(PERCENTAGE DISTRIBUTION)**

	Use of Tax Credit	
Use of CETA Subsidy	Yes	No
Yes	31	23
No	69	78
Total	100	100
Sample Size	(172)	(267)

Note: Percentages may not add to 100 due to rounding.

Summary of Findings

Knowledge and Use of Government Jobs Programs

- The government jobs programs that most businesses have heard of are: CETA On-the-Job Training (87%), Work Incentive (WIN) Tax Credits (79%), Targeted Jobs Tax Credits (73%), CETA-Youth Employment and Training (66%), and CETA-Job Upgrading and Retraining (57%). However, private industry appears to be least familiar with Subminimum Wage Youth Certificates (37%) and the SPEDY Summer Youth Program (22%).
- The three government jobs programs that are used most frequently by private businesses are: the Targeted Jobs Tax Credits (34%), WIN Tax Credits (22%), and CETA-OJT (24%). On the other hand, less than 5% of the businesses surveyed participated in the SPEDY Summer Youth Program (4%) or the Subminimum Wage Youth Certificate Program (3%).

Use of Targeted Jobs Tax Credits (TJTC)

- Trade businesses use the TJTC most frequently, while service firms use them least frequently. Six out of 10 (63%) trade firms use the TJTC, compared to four out of 10 manufacturing (39%) and finance (39%) firms and one out of four service (23%) and "other" (24%) businesses.
- Targeted Jobs Tax Credits are used most frequently by businesses that are small (50-99 employees), in suburban areas, and have high proportions of employees 16-24 years old. Half (47%) of the small businesses use the TJTC, compared to two-fifths of medium-sized (38%) and large (40%) businesses. Almost half (45%) of the suburban firms use the TJTC, compared to 39% of the central city firms and 32% of the firms in rural/exurban areas. Six out of 10 (57%) businesses with 10% or more teenage employees use the TJTC, compared to only two out of 10 (22%) businesses with less than 2% of teenagers. About half (46%) of the businesses with 25% or more young adult employees use the TJTC, compared to only three out of 10 (31%) firms with less than 15% of young adult employees.

Use of Work Incentive (WIN) Tax Credits

- Use of WIN Tax Credits in the private sector varies little by industry. Service (31%) and manufacturing (27%) firms are about as likely as trade (25%) and finance (25%) firms to use WIN credits. It is only among the "other" industries (i.e., agriculture, mining, construction, and transportation) that only a tiny fraction (9%) of the firms use the WIN tax credits.
- Utilization of WIN tax credits also varies little by size or location of business. Large businesses (31%) are about as likely as medium-sized

(23%) and small (25%) firms to use WIN credits. Similarly, central city (25%) are just as likely as suburban (26%) or rural/exurban (24%) firms to use these credits.
- Firms with high proportions of young workers are much more likely to use WIN tax credits than firms with small proportions of youths. Three out of 10 (31%) businesses with 10% or more teenage employees use WIN credits, compared to two out of 10 (19%) firms with less than 2% teenage employees. Similarly, while only 15% of the firms with less than 15% of young adult employees use WIN tax credits, twice as many (32%) of the firms with 25% of more young adult workers use WIN tax credits.

Use of CETA On-The-Job (OJT) Training

- CETA-OJT programs were used most frequently by service firms and used least frequently by "other" businesses. Four out of 10 (42%) service businesses participated in the OJT program, compared to only two out of 10 manufacturing (24%), trade (21%), and finance (22%) firms and only one out of 10 (11%) "other" businesses.
- One-third (34%) of the large businesses participated in the OJT program compared to about one-fourth of the small (28%) and medium-sized (24%) establishments.
- About three out of 10 firms in central cities (29%), suburbs (26%), and rural/exurban (29%) areas participated in the CETA-OJT program.
- Firms with small proportions of young workers tended to participate in the CETA-OJT program less frequently than firms with high proportions. Only 20% of the firms with less than 2% of teenagers participated in the program, compared to 26% of the firms with 10% or more teenage employees. However, firms with less than 15% of young adult employees are only less likely (26%) than firms with 25% or more young adults (29%) to have participated in the CETA-OJT program.

8
Employer Attitudes toward
Youth Wage Subsidies

One of the most controversial issues in the national debate about youth unemployment is whether or not there should be a subminimum wage differential for young people. A number of economic analysts contend that the minimum wage denies disproportionate employment opportunities to young people in general, and minority youth in particular, because employers are unwilling to pay them the same wages as more highly skilled workers.

Findings from the extensive research conducted on the impact of minimum wages on youth employment have been inconsistent and contradictory. While some studies reveal that the minimum wage has a negative impact on youth employment, others indicate that it does not. The most inconclusive results have emerged with respect to the impact of the minimum wage on minority youth employment. Moreover, a major deficiency of almost all of these studies has been the failure to assess the effects of existing legal subminimum wage differentials on the employment of students and other young workers.

On the other hand, there has been little systematic research on the attitudes of *national* samples of employers toward subminimum wage differentials and on the extent to which wage subsidies would be an inducement for them to hire more young people. In order to fill some of the void in this area, this survey asked employers these questions:

1. What effect do you think a subminimum wage differential for youth will have on industry's hiring of youth?
2. Would your company be willing to hire more minority youths if offered a wage subsidy of 50%? (This question was repeated for wage subsidies of 75% and of 100%.)

Attitudes toward Subminimum Wage Differentials

Interestingly, employers are divided as to the probable impact of a subminimum wage differential for youth. While over half (57%) feel

65

that a differential would increase the number of jobs for youth, 40% think that it would have no effect. Only 3% think that it would decrease employment for young people (see Figure 8.1).

FIGURE 8.1
EMPLOYERS' ATTITUDES TOWARD THE EFFECT OF THE
SUBMINIMUM WAGE DIFFERENTIAL ON HIRING OF YOUTHS

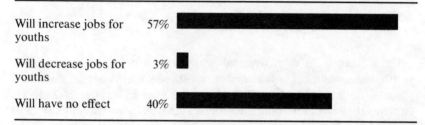

Will increase jobs for youths   57%

Will decrease jobs for youths   3%

Will have no effect   40%

As might be expected, employers in the two industrial sectors with the highest proportions of young employees—trade and services—are much more likely to think that a subminimum wage differential would increase jobs for youth than are employers in other sectors. While three-fifths of the trade (63%) and service (61%) employers think that a differential would increase jobs for youth, 38% of the service firms and 33% of the trade firms believe that it would have no effect. On the other hand, about half of the manufacturing (48%) and finance (43%) employers think that a subminimum wage differential would increase jobs for youth, while the remaining half of manufacturing (51%) and finance (55%) firms think that it would not have any impact (see Table 8.1).

Size of business is not directly related to attitudes toward a subminimum wage differential. Employers in moderate size businesses (60%) are more likely to feel that a differential would increase jobs for youth than are employers in small (53%) or large (52%) businesses (see Table 8.2).

Unexpectedly, the proportion of teenagers employed is not significantly related to employer attitudes toward a differential. In fact, employers with a low proportion of teenagers are only slightly less likely (54%) than employers with moderate (59%) or high (58%) proportions of teenage employees to think that a subminimum wage differential would increase jobs for young people (see Table 8.3).

However, employer attitudes toward a youth differential are related to the proportion of young adult employees—but in an unexpected direction. Employers with low proportions (0-14%) of young adults are most likely (62%) to think that a youth differential would increase jobs

TABLE 8.1
EMPLOYERS' ATTITUDES TOWARD THE SUBMINIMUM WAGE DIFFERENTIAL, BY TYPE OF BUSINESS (PERCENTAGE DISTRIBUTION)

Attitude Toward Subminimum Wage	Business				
	Manufacturing	Trade	Finance	Service	Other [a]
Increase Jobs for Youths	48	63	43	61	48
Decrease Jobs for Youths	1	5	2	1	- [b]
Have No Effect	51	33	55	38	52
Total	100	100	100	100	100
Sample Size	(83)	(126)	(44)	(141)	(31)

a. Other businesses include agriculture, mining, construction, and transportation.
b. There were no answers in this category.

TABLE 8.2
EMPLOYERS' ATTITUDES TOWARD THE SUBMINIMUM WAGE DIFFERENTIAL, BY SIZE OF BUSINESS (PERCENTAGE DISTRIBUTION)

Attitude Toward Subminimum Wage	Size		
	Small (1-99)	Medium (100-249)	Large (250 & over)
Increase Jobs for Youths	53	60	52
Decrease Jobs for Youths	1	2	4
Have No Effect	45	38	44
Total	100	100	100
Sample Size	(79)	(204)	(142)

Note: Percentages may not add to 100 due to rounding.

for youth, while employers with high proportions (25% and over) of young adult employees are least likely (54%) to feel this way (see Table 8.4).

As might be expected, firms that have used the subminimum wage certificates for students are more likely to think that a differential

TABLE 8.3

**EMPLOYERS' ATTITUDES TOWARD THE SUBMINIMUM WAGE
DIFFERENTIAL, BY PROPORTION OF TEENAGE HIRES
(PERCENTAGE DISTRIBUTION)**

Attitude Toward Subminimum Wage Differential	Proportion of Teenage Hires		
	Low (0-1%)	Moderate (2-9%)	High (10% & over)
Increase Jobs for Youths	54	59	58
Decrease Jobs for Youths	3	1	4
Have No Effect	43	40	38
Total	100	100	100
Sample Size	(143)	(157)	(186)

Note: Percentages may not add to 100 due to rounding.

TABLE 8.4

**EMPLOYERS' ATTITUDES TOWARD THE SUBMINIMUM WAGE
DIFFERENTIAL FOR YOUTHS, BY PROPORTION OF
YOUNG ADULT HIRES
(PERCENTAGE DISTRIBUTION)**

Attitude Toward Subminimum Wage	Proportion of Young Adult Hires		
	Low (0-14%)	Moderate (15-24%)	High (25% & over)
Increase Jobs for Youths	62	55	54
Decrease Jobs for Youths	1	1	5
Have No Effect	37	43	-
Total	100	100	100
Sample Size	(145)	(134)	(207)

Note: Percentages may not add to 100 due to rounding.

would increase jobs for youth than are firms that have not used those certificates. Three-fourths (73%) of the employers that have used the subminimum wage certificates think that a differential would create more jobs for young people, compared to 58% of the employers that have not used the certificates (see Table 8.5).

TABLE 8.5
EMPLOYERS' ATTITUDES TOWARD THE SUBMINIMUM WAGE
DIFFERENTIAL, BY USE OF SUBMINIMUM WAGE CERTIFICATES
(PERCENTAGE DISTRIBUTION)

Attitude Toward Subminimum Wage	Use of Subminimum Wage Certificates	
	Yes	No
Increase Jobs for Youths	73	58
Decrease Jobs for Youths	$-$ a	2
Have No Effect	27	40
Total	100	100
Sample Size	(15)	(390)

a. There were no answers in this category.
Note: Percentages may not add to 100 due to rounding.

In sum, the employers most likely to think that a subminimum wage differential would increase jobs for youth are in trade and services; are medium-sized (100-249 employees); have low proportions of young adult employees; and have used the subminimum wage certificates.

Minority Hiring at Various Wage Subsidies

When a national sample of employers was asked whether they would hire more minority youths if offered various wage subsidies, half of them failed to answer one way or another. However, of those that did respond, half said they would hire more minority youth, while the other half said they would not—regardless of the level of the wage subsidy! For example, 26% of the employers said they would hire more minority youth if offered a wage subsidy of 100%, but virtually the same proportion (28%) said they would hire more minority youths if offered a 50% wage subsidy (see Table 8.6).

Figure 8.2 depicts the similarity of employer attitudes at various wage subsidies (nonresponding employers are excluded). Thus, while 47% of the responding employers indicated that they would be willing to hire more minority youth at a 100% wage subsidy, an equal proportion (48%) said that they would hire more minority youths at a 50% subsidy.

The willingness of employers to hire more minority youths at a 100%

FIGURE 8.2
PERCENTAGE OF BUSINESSES WILLING TO HIRE MORE MINORITY YOUTHS IF OFFERED WAGE SUBSIDIES

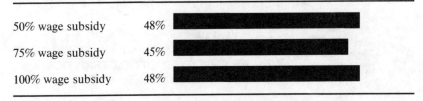

50% wage subsidy	48%
75% wage subsidy	45%
100% wage subsidy	48%

TABLE 8.6
WILLINGNESS OF EMPLOYERS TO HIRE MORE MINORITY YOUTH, BY LEVEL OF WAGE SUBSIDY

Willingness of Employers to Hire Youth	Level of Wage Subsidy		
	50%	75%	100%
Total Sample (No.)	535	535	535
Total Percent	100%	100%	100%
Yes	28	24	26
No	31	30	29
No answer	42	46	45

wage subsidy is related to various characteristics of businesses in Table 8.7. The data (which exclude nonrespondents) reveal that manufacturing employers (36%) are less willing to hire more minority youths at a 100% subsidy, while employers in finance (61%) and services (57%) are more willing. And, medium-sized businesses (52%) are more likely to hire more minority youth at a full wage subsidy, while small businesses (44%) are less willing.

Location is not a major correlate of the willingness of employers to hire minority youth at a 100% wage subsidy. Employers in the suburbs (46%) and central cities (50%) are equally willing to hire minority youth at a full subsidy, while those in rural areas are only slightly less willing (44%). Moreover, the same proportions (about half) of employers are willing to hire more minority youth at a 100% subsidy, regardless of their regional location.

However, the proportion of teenage employees is strongly correlated with employer willingness to hire minority youth at 100% wage subsidy. While half of the employers with moderate (51%) and high (54%) proportions of teenagers are willing to hire these youth at a full subsidy, only 36% of the firms with low proportions of teenagers are

TABLE 8.7
WILLINGNESS OF EMPLOYERS TO HIRE MORE MINORITY YOUTH AT 100% WAGE SUBSIDY, BY EMPLOYER CHARACTERISTICS (PERCENT WILLING TO HIRE MINORITY YOUTH)

A. Type of Business

(47)[a] Manufacturing	(70)[a] Trade	(23)[a] Finance	(84)[a] Service	(25)[a] Other[b]
36%	51%	61%	57%	32%

B. Size of Business

(39) Under 100 Employees	(130) 100-249	(74) 250 and over
44%	52%	47%

C. Location of Business

(48) Northeast	(77) Northcentral	(72) South	(57) West
50%	48%	46%	54%

E. Proportion of Teenagers Employed

(86) Low (0-1%)	(109) Moderate (2-9%)	(98) High (10% and over)
36%	51%	54%

D. Proportion of Young Adults Employed

(87) Low (0-14%)	(86) Moderate (15-24%)	(120) High (25% and over)
46%	49%	48%

a. Numbers in parentheses refer to sample sizes in each category.
b. "Other" includes agriculture, mining, construction, and transportation.

willing. On the other hand, the proportion of young adult employees is not correlated with employer willingness to hire. Regardless of their proportion of young adult employees, half of all the businesses are willing to hire more minority youth.

These findings indicate clearly that, contrary to popular belief, the level of wage subsidy is not a significant factor in the willingness of most employers to hire minority youth. It appears that employers who are committed to hiring minority youth will maintain that commitment, regardless of a wage subsidy.

Summary of Findings

Attitudes toward Subminimum Wage Youth Differentials

- Employers are split in their assessment of the impact of a subminimum wage youth differential. While over half (57%) of all employers think that it will increase jobs for young people, less than half (43%) think it will have no effect (40%) or will decrease (3%) the number of jobs available for young people.
- Trade and service firms are more likely than businesses in other industries to think that a subminimum wage differential will increase jobs for youths. Three out of 10 trade (63%) and service (61%) firms feel it will increase jobs for youths, compared to about half of the manufacturing (48%), finance (43%), and "other" (48%) businesses. Or, while the majority of manufacturing, finance, and "other" businesses think that a youth differential will have no effect or will decrease jobs for young people, a majority of trade and service firms think it will increase jobs for youths.
- Over half of all businesses think that a youth subminimum differential will increase jobs for youths whether they are small (53%), medium-sized (60%), or large (52%). Nevertheless, half of the small (47%) and large (48%) businesses and two-fifths of the medium-sized (40%) firms think that a youth differential will not increase jobs for young people.
- Interestingly, employer attitudes about subminimum differentials are not related to their proportion of teenage employees. Over half of all businesses think that a subminimum differential will increase jobs for youths, whether they have a low (54%), moderate (59%), or high (58%) proportion of teenagers employed. On the other hand, four out of 10 businesses think it will have no effect or will decrease jobs for young people, regardless of their proportion of teenage employees.
- However, there is some relationship between attitudes toward youth differentials and the proportion of young adult employees. Six out of 10 businesses with low (62%) proportions of young adults think that subminimum wage differentials will increase jobs for young people as

do five out of 10 businesses with moderate (55%) and high (54%) proportions of young adult workers. Nevertheless, four out of 10 firms think such differentials will not increase jobs for young people, regardless of their proportion of young adult employees.

- As might be expected, attitudes toward youth differentials are directly related to the extent to which firms make use of subminimum wage certificates. Among firms that make use of the subminimum wage certificates, three-fourths (73%) think that youth differentials will increase jobs for young people, while one-fourth (27%) think it will not increase jobs for youth. Among businesses that do not use the subminimum wage certificates, six out of 10 (58%) think it will increase jobs for young people, while four out of 10 (42%) think it will have no effect or will decrease jobs for young people.

Minority Hiring at Various Wage Subsidies

- The willingness of employers to hire minority youths is not affected by the level of wage subsidy offered. Three out of 10 businesses are not willing to hire more minority youths, whether they are offered wage subsidies of 50% (31%), 75% (30%), or 100% (29%). One out of four businesses are willing to hire more minority youths, whether they are offered wage subsidies of 50% (28%), 75% (24%), or 100 percent (26%). And four out of 10 businesses refuse to answer one way or the other.
- Among those businesses that answered, they are split about their willingness to hire more minority youths, regardless of the level of wage subsidy offered. Half are willing to hire more minority youths, while the other half are not willing. For example, at a 100% subsidy, 52% of all businesses surveyed are not willing to hire minority youths, while 48% are willing. At a 75% subsidy, 55% are not willing to hire minority youth, while 45% are willing. And at a 50% subsidy, 52% are not willing to hire minority youths, while 48% are willing.

Minority Hiring at 100% Wage Subsidy

- Finance and service firms are more willing to hire minority youths at a 100% wage subsidy than are manufacturing and "other" businesses. Six out of 10 finance (61%) and service (57%) businesses are willing to hire more minority youth, compared to only three out of 10 manufacturing (36%) and "other" (32%) establishments.
- The willingness of employers to hire more minority youths at a 100% wage subsidy does not vary significantly by size, location, or region of business. Medium-sized (52%) and large (47%) firms are only slightly more willing than small (44%) businesses. Businesses in central cities (50%) and suburbs (46%) are only slightly more willing

than those in rural/exurban (44%) areas. And businesses in the West
(54%) and Northeast (50%) are only slightly more willing than firms
in the South (46%) and North-Central (48%) regions.

- Willingness to hire more minority youth is directly related to the
  proportion of teenagers employed. About half of the firms with
  moderate (51%) and high (54%) proportions of teenage workers are
  willing to hire more minority youth at a 100% wage subsidy, compared to only one-third of the businesses with low (36%) proportions
  of teenage employees.
- However, willingness to hire more minority youth at a 100% wage
  subsidy is not related to the proportion of young adult employees.
  Firms with low (46%) proportions of young adult workers are about
  as willing to hire more minority youth as businesses with moderate
  (49%) and high (48%) proportions of young adult workers.

9

Improving the Employability of Youths: Roles of Industry and Schools

There is some empirical evidence that private-sector employers support a role for business in preparing young people for the world of work.[1] For example, the vice-president's roundtables made it clear that employers were interested in enhancing relationships with educational institutions to jointly prepare youths for the labor force. Several action strategies were identified, which included:

- Short-term work experience of a career exploratory type.
- Meetings with educators to discuss a range of vocational and educational issues.
- Assistance to educators in developing jobs-related basic curricula (career education) or specific trade curricula.
- Lectures, career days, and similar informational exercises.
- Work sampling for teachers and guidance counselors in which these educational professionals would spend time inside employers experiencing a variety of occupations and work environments.
- Specific skill training, either at the employer or in vocational schools.[2]

Employers at the roundtable also expressed a preference for dealing with schools rather than CETA in the joint preparation of kids, although they expected the schools to take the initiative. Their reasons being: (1) schools have longevity and permanence, (2) schools are the appropriate basic institution that serve all children, and (3) schools are more credible than CETA.

In addition, these employers stressed a need for more communication as a first step towards meaningful connections between business and schools. Although private industry councils (PICS) were favorably described, it was noted that the structure was not broad based enough for interaction with the educational sector. The employers also admonished that the nature of an ongoing relationship between the private and education sector would "vary from industry to industry and from large to small companies."[3]

Although several activities for improving the employability of youths have been identified by experts on youth employment, we sought in the employer survey to *prioritize* business views on the specific roles that private industry and schools should take on in the preparation and training of young people for the world of work. Next we present the employers' rankings on these roles for youths in general. In the last section, we present employers' answers to the question: What would you recommend as an effective means to hire *more minority youths?*

The Role of Schools

Firms were given a list of three efforts that schools could emphasize to improve the employability of young people: (1) concentrate on basic skills; (2) provide practical world of work orientation; and (3) involve industry in curriculum development. The employers were then asked to rank each role as "very important," "somewhat important," or "not important." We found that nine out of 10 firms (92%) ranked "concentration on basic skills" by schools as very important to improve the employability of youths. By contrast, almost four out of 10 (36%) companies ranked "providing students with practical world-of-work orientation" as very important, while only four percent ranked "involving industry in curriculum development" as very important (see Table 9.1).

The Role of Private Industry

Firms were asked to rank the following five efforts by private industry to improve the employability of youths as "very important," "somewhat important," or "not important": (1) provide short-term work experience for students; (2) provide more skill training on the job; (3) create stronger linkages with job placement agencies; (4) aid education in developing job-related curriculum; and (5) create nontraditional apprenticeship programs. We found that almost six out of ten (58%) of the employers ranked the "provision of more skills training on the job" as very important. Half (50%) of the companies rated "provision of short-term work experiences for students" and "aid education in developing job-related curriculum" as very important. On the other hand, approximately four out of 10 (37%) firms rated the "creation of nontraditional apprenticeship programs" (e.g., computer programming) as "very important"; and three out of 10 (29%) ranked "creating

TABLE 9.1
EMPLOYERS' RANKING OF HOW SCHOOLS CAN IMPROVE
EMPLOYABILITY OF YOUTHS
(PERCENTAGE DISTRIBUTION)

	Item		
Rank	Concentrate on Basic Skills	Provide Practical World of Work Orientation	Involve Industry in Curriculum Development
Very Important	92	36	4
Somewhat Important	7	51	52
Not Important	1	13	12
Total	100	100	100
Sample Size	(513)	(503)	(491)

Note: Percentages may not add to 100 due to rounding.

strong linkages with job placement agencies" as very important (see Table 9.2).

Minority Youths

More effective means to hire more minority youths was a key issue in the employer survey. The participating firms were asked for recommendations to bolster the numbers of minority youth hires. Their recommendations revolved around four categories: (1) basic skills training; (2) orientation to the world of work; (3) basic education; and (4) need for better transportation. Below are some typical statements employers made regarding these recommendations:

Basic Skills Training
   1. "Development of good work skills through school programs."
   2. "Need for better job-related training."
Orientation to World of Work
   1. "Better preparation for world of work—neatness, politeness, positive approach."

TABLE 9.2
EMPLOYERS' RANKING OF HOW BUSINESS CAN IMPROVE THE
EMPLOYABILITY OF YOUTHS
(PERCENTAGE DISTRIBUTION)

Rank	Provide Short Term Work Experience for Students	Provide More Skill Training On the Job	Create Stronger Linkages With Job Placement Agencies	Aid Education in Developing Job-Related Curriculum	Create Non-traditional Apprenticeship Programs
			Item		
Very Important	50	58	29	50	37
Somewhat Important	41	40	48	41	52
Not Important	9	2	23	9	11
Total	100	100	100	100	100
Sample Size	(499)	(501)	(497)	(492)	(486)

Note: Percentages may not add to 100 due to rounding.

2. "Youths should be well-versed in what it takes to get and hold a job—attendance, punctuality, knowledge of job opportunities."
3. "Development of work ethic, improve dependability, and willingness to work."

Basic Education
1. "Send us youths who can read, write, and do simple math."
2. "Improve communication skills."
3. "Cultural (street) language; lack of verbal and mathematical skills adversely affect hiring rate—education and "mainstreaming" are the best long-range solutions."

Transportation
1. "Transportation costs are a factor in our ability to hire—bus passes would be a help."
2. "Youths need better transportation to jobs from areas of the cities where most minorities are concentrated."

Thus, the employers stressed the need for better industry-related skill training, the development of a work ethic and positive work attitudes, mastery of the three Rs, and easier physical access to jobs for minority youths.

Employers also emphasized the role that schools, community-based organizations, and private industry should play to facilitate the employment of more minority youths. Schools, the employers recommend, should do a better job of grooming minority youths for industry through basic education, effective training programs, and systematic referral from technical training programs. Community-based organizations, to complement the role of schools, should engage in more active promotion and referral of qualified applicants to businesses. Private industry, on the other hand, has a responsibility to become better educated to the needs of minority youths and to become more involved in jobs programs.

Summary of Findings

Ways for Schools to Increase Youth Employability

• The overwhelming majority of businesses surveyed place top priority on schools making youth more employable by concentrating on basic reading, writing, and math skills. Nine out of 10 (92%) firms think it is "very important" for schools to concentrate on the basics, 7% think it is "somewhat important," while only 1% think it is "not important."
• Providing students with practical world-of-work orientation was the

second most important way that businesses felt that schools could increase the employability of young people. One-third (36%) of the firms think that such practical orientation is "very important," half (51%) think it is "somewhat important," and 13% think that it is "not important."

- One-fourth (26%) of all businesses surveyed think that it is "very important" to involve industry in developing work-related curricula, half (52%) think it is "somewhat important," and 12% think it is "not important."

Ways for Businesses to Increase Youth Employability

- Businesses place the higher priority on providing skill training on the job as an effective means for private industry to increase the employability of young people and the lowest priority on linking up with job development and placement agencies. Five out of 10 firms consider it "very important" for businesses to provide OJT skill training (58%), to provide short-term work experience for youths (50%), and to help educators develop job-related curricula (50%), while 37% think it is "very important" to create nontraditional apprenticeship programs and 29% think it is "very important" to create stronger linkages with job development and placement agencies.

Notes

1. Seymour Lusterman and Harriet Gorlin, *Educating Students for Work: Some Business Roles* (New York: Conference Board, 1980).
2. Erik P. Butler and James Darr, *Research on Youth Employment and Employability Development: Educator and Employer Perspectives* (Waltham, Mass.: Brandeis University Press, May 1980), pp. 9-10.
3. Ibid., pp. 36-37.

10
The Labor Market: Projections for the Future

Prophetic utterances about the labor market of the future abound from diverse sources. Such forecasting is absolutely essential if labor market demands and job training are to mesh smoothly. Without good forecasting, the probability is heightened that an oversupply of workers will occur in occupations where demand has shrunk. Consequently, it is important to define the job opportunities that young people will have in the future to assist them in making good career plans.[1]

Forecasters agree that the "belching smokestacks" of the industrial age are rapidly passing. According to futurist Alvin Toffler, the coming "third wave" society will not be characterized by a blue-collar way of life but instead the new system will be characterized by a new economy (customized production and small manufacturing), new values, work habits, and attitudes. Although the three Rs, repetitiveness, and fixed hierarchies are basic to a factory economy, the "third wave" culture will require innovative individuals with good judgment and the ability to improvise. Moreover, training in the "third wave" educational system will require entrepreneurial skills and computer literacy.[2]

What will be the status of entry level jobs by the end of the 1980s? Business trade papers have consistently predicted that entry level jobs will decrease during the eighties as the new technology really "takes hold" with electronic mail, automated warehouses, computerized information processing, robotics, and so on.[3] Expanding technology, however, is but one thread that threatens the frayed fabric of youth employment in the future. The number of entry level jobs may also shrink because of replacement through higher entry requirements. Thus, technological innovations may reduce the number of unskilled entry level jobs while available jobs become increasingly more complex and professional.[4]

Shifts in the demographic composition of the workforce during the decade of the eighties will also impact the outlook for youth employment. Employers are likely to face wider opportunities to fill declining entry-level jobs with larger pools of women, minority adults, senior

citizens, and immigrants. These competing groups may vie for shrink-
ing entry-level positions as well as professional and managerial jobs.
Much of the rate increase for white women, though, is expected to
occur in professional and managerial work roles.[5]

Based on our survey, what are private employers' projections for the
growth of entry-level unskilled, semiskilled, and skilled jobs over the
next five years? We now present employers' expectations for job
growth by type of business, size of business, location, and region.

Unskilled Jobs

When analyzed by type of business, we found that over half of the
manufacturing, trade, finance, and service establishments expect that
the number of entry-level unskilled jobs will remain *constant* over the
next five years. Nearly half (47%) of "other" businesses (mining,
construction, agriculture, transportation) predict that the growth of
unskilled jobs will remain the same over the next five years (see Table
10.1). Similarly, the majority of all size businesses—small (54%),
medium (56%), and large (65%)—project that the growth of unskilled
jobs will probably remain the same over the next five years. On the

TABLE 10.1
EXPECTATIONS FOR GROWTH OF UNSKILLED JOBS OVER THE NEXT
FIVE YEARS, BY TYPE OF BUSINESS
(PERCENTAGE DISTRIBUTION)

Expectations	Business				
	Manufacturing	Trade	Finance	Service	Other[a]
Probably Increase	37	20	20	24	24
Probably Decrease	13	19	17	13	29
Probably Remain the Same	51	61	63	63	47
Total	100	100	100	100	100
Sample Size	(79)	(115)	(35)	(142)	(34)

a. Other businesses include mining, agriculture, construction, and transportation.
Note: Percentages may not add to 100 due to rounding.

other hand, only three out of 10 small, medium, and large firms expect that the number of unskilled jobs will increase over the next five years.

When analyzed by location, approximately three out of five businesses in each location (central city/town, suburbs, rural/exurbs) project that the number of unskilled jobs will remain the same over the next five years. The same pattern holds true for firms in each region—Northeast, North-Central, West, and South. Three out of five establishments in each region expect the growth of unskilled jobs to remain the same over the next five years. Increases in the number of unskilled jobs, however, are projected by more firms located in the West and South than in other regions—30 percent of these firms expect an increase (see Tables I, J, K in Appendix D).

Based on these data employers appear to be more conservative in their expectations concerning the decrease of entry-level jobs, at least for the next five years, than the prevailing forecast literature suggests. Private employers in our survey did not foresee gross shrinkages in entry-level unskilled jobs in the near future; rather, the majority belief is that the number of unskilled jobs will remain constant over the next five years.

Semiskilled Jobs

The majority of the manufacturing (53%), trade (64%), finance (51%), and service (60%) establishments expect that the growth of semiskilled jobs will remain the same over the next five years (see Table 10.2). On the question of semiskilled job growth, "other" businesses (mining, agriculture, construction, transportation), however, are equally divided between those expecting the number of semiskilled jobs to remain the same (43%) and those expecting such jobs to increase (43%). Over half of small (58%), medium (55%), and large (60%) firms expect growth of semiskilled jobs to remain constant over the next five years. By contrast, virtually three out of 10 small, medium, and large establishments expect semiskilled jobs to increase over the next five years.

When analyzed by location of business, over half of the firms located in central cities/towns (55%), suburbs (65%), and rural/exurbs (51%) project that the number of semiskilled jobs will remain constant over the next five years. Proportionately more firms located in central cities/towns (37%) and rural/exurbs (41%), however, anticipate the number of semiskilled jobs to increase over the next five years compared to only 26% of the establishments located in the suburbs. By region, the majority of firms in the Northeast, North-Central, West, and South

TABLE 10.2
EXPECTATIONS FOR GROWTH OF SEMISKILLED JOBS OVER THE
NEXT FIVE YEARS, BY TYPE OF BUSINESS
(PERCENTAGE DISTRIBUTION)

| Expectations | Business | | | | |
	Manufacturing	Trade	Finance	Service	Other[a]
Probably Increase	40	29	38	35	43
Probably Decrease	7	7	11	6	14
Probably Remain the Same	53	64	51	60	43
Total	100	100	100	100	100
Sample Size	(83)	(120)	(45)	(145)	(37)

a. Other businesses include mining, agriculture, construction, and transportation.
Note: Percentages may not add to 100 due to rounding.

expect the number of semiskilled jobs to remain the same over the next five years. Increases in the number of semiskilled jobs, though, are projected by more firms in the West (42%) and in the South (38%) than in other regions (see Tables L, M, N in Appendix D).

Skilled Jobs

By type of business, all establishments, except for trade, are about equally divided on their projections for the growth of skilled jobs over the next five years. Nearly half of manufacturing (51%), finance (43%), service (50%), and "other" (43%) businesses (mining, construction, agriculture, transportation) estimated that the number of skilled jobs will remain the same. The other half of these firms project that the number of skilled jobs will increase over the next five years—46%, 50%, 48%, and 43%, respectively. The majority of trade establishments (57%), however, expect skilled jobs to remain the same (see table 10.3). Virtually half of small (55%), medium (50%), and large (50%) businesses anticipate that skilled jobs will remain constant over the next five years. By contrast, four out of 10 small, medium, and large businesses expect skilled jobs to increase over the next five years.

When broken down by location of business, the majority of employers in the suburbs (58%) expect skilled jobs to remain the same over the

TABLE 10.3
**EXPECTATIONS FOR GROWTH OF SKILLED JOBS OVER THE NEXT
FIVE YEARS, BY TYPE OF BUSINESS
(PERCENTAGE DISTRIBUTION)**

Expectations	Business				
	Manufacturing	Trade	Finance	Service	Other[a]
Probably Increase	46	34	50	48	43
Probably Decrease	4	10	7	2	14
Probably Remain the Same	51	57	43	50	43
Total	100	100	100	100	100
Sample Size	(83)	(133)	(44)	(149)	(37)

a. Other businesses include mining, agriculture, construction, and transportation.
Note: Percentages may not add to 100 due to rounding.

next five years. But about half of the employers in rural/exurbs (52%) expect skilled jobs to increase. Employers in central cities/towns are nearly equally divided on the issue of skilled job growth over the next five years. Half (50%) believe that the number of skilled jobs will remain constant, while 44% expect that the number of skilled jobs will increase. By region, approximately half of the firms located in the Northeast (54%), North-Central (54%), and South (52%) project the number of skilled jobs to remain the same over the next five years. By contrast, four out of 10 firms located in these regions expect skilled jobs to increase. Half of firms in the West (51%), however, expect skilled jobs to increase over the next five years (see Tables O, P, Q in Appendix D).

Thus, employers forecast increases in the number of skilled jobs in nearly every *type* of industry over the next five years. By size of business, a fair percentage expect that skilled jobs will expand over the next five years. Increasingly, then, the labor market will demand more complex professional and technical skills to fill professional and technical slots in rural areas, central cities/towns, and, lastly, in suburban locations.

Summary of Findings

Five-Year Projections for Unskilled Jobs

- Contrary to popular belief, the overwhelming majority (84%) of the businesses surveyed do not expect the number of unskilled entry-level jobs in their firms to decline over the next five years. In fact, only two out of 10 (17%) firms anticipate a drop in unskilled jobs, while six out of 10 expect them to remain the same and one out of four (25%) expect their unskilled jobs to increase.
- Eight out of 10 manufacturing (88%), service (87%), finance (83%), and trade (81%) firms expect their unskilled jobs to increase or remain the same, compared to seven out of 10 (71%) "other" businesses.
- Regardless of size, region, or location, most businesses expect no decline in their unskilled jobs. Eight out of 10 small (83%), medium-sized (82%), and large (86%) businesses anticipate their unskilled jobs to increase or remain the same. Similarly high proportions of businesses are in the South (88%), West (83%), Northeast (84%) and North-Central (82%) regions. Moreover, eight out of 10 firms in central cities (82%), suburbs (84%), and rural/exurban (87%) areas expect the number of their unskilled entry-level jobs to increase or remain the same over the next five years.

Five-Year Projections for Semiskilled Jobs

- The overwhelming majority (92%) of businesses expect their semiskilled jobs to increase or remain the same over the next five years. One-third (35%) expect their semiskilled jobs to increase, six out of 10 (57%) expect them to remain the same, and less than one out of 10 (7%) expect them to decline.
- Four out of 10 manufacturing (40%), finance (38%), and "other" (43%) businesses expect their semiskilled jobs to increase, while about half of manufacturing (47%), finance (51%), and "other" (43%) expect them to remain the same.
- About one-third of small (37%), medium-sized (37%), and large (32%) businesses expect their semiskilled jobs to increase, while six out of 10 firms expect them to remain the same.
- Four out of 10 businesses in central cities (37%) and rural/exurban (41%) areas expect their semiskilled jobs to increase, compared to one out of four (26%) firms in the surburbs.
- Four out of 10 businesses in the South (38%) and West (42%) expect their semiskilled jobs to rise, while three out of 10 firms in the Northeast (33%) and North-Central (30%) regions also expect such increases among their semiskilled jobs.

Five-Year Projections for Skilled Jobs

- Almost all (94%) of the businesses surveyed expect their skilled jobs to increase or remain the same over the next five years. Four out of 10 (43%) firms expect their skilled jobs to increase, half (51%) expect them to remain the same, and only 6% expect them to decline.
- About half of the manufacturing (46%), service (48%), and finance (50%) businesses expect their skilled jobs to rise, while most of the remaining half expect them to remain unchanged over the next five years. Only one-third (34%) of the trade and 43% of "other" businesses expect their skilled jobs to increase, while 57% of the trade and 43% of "other" firms expect them to remain unchanged.
- The future projections of skilled jobs do not vary by size of business. Four out of 10 businesses expect their skilled jobs to increase over the next five years whether they are small (39%), medium-sized (45%), or large (44%).
- Firms in rural/exurban (52%) areas are more likely than firms in central cities (44%) or suburbs (34%) to expect an increase in their skilled jobs, while about half of the businesses in each of these three locations expect their skilled jobs to remain the same.
- Half of the firms in the West (51%) expect their skilled jobs to increase over the next five years, compared to four out of 10 firms in the South (43%), Northeast (43%) and North-Central (40%) regions.

Notes

1. The White House, A Summary Report of the Vice-President's Task Force on Youth Employment (Washington, D.C.: The White House, 1980), p. 36
2. Alvin Toffler, "A Look at the Future," National Urban League Conference, New Orleans, 1983.
3. Ibid., p. 5.
4. Erik P. Butler and James Darr, Research on Youth Employment and Employability Development: Educator and Employer Perspectives (Waltham, Mass.: Brandeis University Press, May 1980), p. 33.
5. Paul W. Schewegler, "Human Resources: A Profile and Design for the 80's" (Redondo Beach, Calif.: Industrial Relations, TRW Defense and Space Systems Group, 1979).

11
Conclusions and Recommendations

The persistent high level of unemployment among young people continues to be an issue of major national importance today. Jobless rates among teenagers are generally five times that of workers 25 years and over, while unemployment rates among youth 20-24 years old are about 2.5 times as high. This problem is especially acute among minority youth whose jobless rates are usually two or three times higher than those of white youth. In 1983, for example, one out of every two black teenagers were officially unemployed, compared to one out of every five white teenagers. Such unabating levels of joblessness—even in times of prosperity—deprive thousands of young people of vital work experience and skill development needed to enhance their employment opportunities as adults.

Thus, a major question of national concern is, "How can we get private industry to significantly increase opportunities for entry-level employment of young people?" In order to effectively increase private-sector jobs for young people in the future, however, it is instructive to have systematic knowledge about past and current experiences and attitudes of employers concerning the performance of young workers.

Although an extensive amount of research has been conducted on numerous aspects of labor market experiences of young people, there are few *nationwide* studies of the attitudes, practices, and policies of private employers toward hiring youths. Much of the research in this area has been based on case studies of only a few firms or on purposively-selected companies in a limited number of geographic locations. And no study, for example, has asked national samples of employers about their attitudes toward such controversial topics as subminimum wage differentials and wage subsidies as inducements for hiring young people in general and minority youth in particular.

This study attempts to fill some of these voids by interviewing a random cross-section of 535 private employers across the nation during the winter of 1981-82 about the following issues:

1. In which industries and occupations are young people most concentrated?
2. What guidelines are used in hiring young people?
3. What opportunities for advancement are provided young workers in private industry?
4. How do employers rate the job performance of youths relative to that of adults?
5. What are the recent hiring patterns of minority youth in private industry?
6. To what extent have private employers participated in major government jobs programs (such as on-the-job training, jobs tax credits, and subminimum wage youth certificates)?
7. What impact do employers think that a subminimum wage differential will have on employment opportunities for young people?
8. To what extent would employers be willing to hire more minority youths at wage subsidies of either 100%, 75%, or 50%?
9. What do employers think are the most effective ways for schools and for businesses to increase the employability of young people?
10. What projections do employers have for their unskilled, semiskilled, and skilled jobs over the next five years?

The major findings and recommendations related to each of those 10 issues are summarized as follows:

Industrial and Occupational Representation

1. *Need for strategies that facilitate the mobility of young workers into long-term, higher-paying occupations in expanding industries.* Although youths are more likely to work in expanding (e.g., trade, finance, and service) rather than contracting (e.g., manufacturing) industries, they are still disproportionately concentrated in short-term lower-paying jobs.

Guidelines for Hiring Youth

2. *Need for private industry to adopt more flexible guidelines that increase opportunities for teenagers to secure full-time entry-level positions.* Young adults are more likely than teenagers to be hired for entry-level jobs and for positions that require some experience. However, teenagers are more likely than young adults to be hired for part-time jobs.

Opportunities for Advancement

3. *Need to increase advancement opportunities for young workers, especially in service firms and in medium-sized and large businesses.* Young workers have the most opportunities for advancement in trade and finance establishments and the least opportuni-

ties in service firms. Teenagers have greater advancement opportunities in small rather than medium-size or large businesses.

Rating the Job Performance of Youth

4. *Need to disseminate more widely the fact that most employers think that in most areas young workers perform as well as adults.* More than six out of 10 employers think that the job performance of young people, 20-24 years old, is the same as or better than that of mature adults, 25 years and older. And half of them think that punctuality and discipline among teenagers is no worse than among mature adults.

Recent Hiring Patterns of Minority Youth

5. *Need to increase the number of private industry-initiated special jobs programs for minority youths.* Less than 1% of the businesses surveyed currently have jobs programs targeted to minority young people. Nevertheless, minority youths are more likely to be hired in expanding (e.g., trade, finance and service) industries than in contracting (e.g., manufacturing) ones.

Participation in Government Jobs Programs

6. *Need for information efforts that make more employers aware of the variety of government programs available to increase employment opportunities for young people.* While three out of four (73%) employers surveyed are familiar with the Targeted Jobs Tax Credits (TJTC), only four out of 10 (37%) have ever heard of the Subminimum Wage Youth Certificate Program. Moreover, while one-third (34%) of the employers have used the TJTC, only 3% have used Subminimum Wage Youth Certificates.

Impact of Subminimum Wage Youth Differential

7. *Further studies are needed to determine why almost half of all employers surveyed do not think that a subminimum wage differential will increase job opportunities for young people.* While a plurality (57%) of all employers surveyed believe that a subminimum wage differential would increase employment opportunities for young people, almost half (43%) do not think a differential will increase jobs for youth.

Minority Hiring at Various Wage Subsidies

8. *Need to disseminate more widely the fact that the willingness of employers to hire minority youths is based more on their commitment to provide opportunities for disadvantaged young people than on the level of wage subsidy offered.* About half of all employers surveyed are willing to hire more minority youth, while

the other half are not—whether they are offered wage subsidies of 50%, 75%, or 100%.

Ways to Increase Employability of Youth

9. *There needs to be greater concentration on the basics in school and more skill training on the job in private industry in order to enhance the employability of youth.* Most employers place top priority on schools concentrating on the basics (i.e., reading, writing, and arithmetic) and on private industry providing more skill training on the job as effective ways to increase youth employability.

Five-Year Projections of Jobs

10. *Since the overwhelming majority of employers do not expect their unskilled jobs to decline over the next five years, special educational and training efforts must be adopted to prevent young workers from being largely confined to them.* Only two out of 10 (17%) of all employers surveyed expect their unskilled jobs to decline over the next five years, while six out of 10 expect them to remain about the same, and one out of four expect the number to increase.

Appendix A:
Description of the Universe—The EEO-1 List

EEOC's EEO-1 data base was used. The EEO-1 was the best quality list for its cost when compared with other available lists (i.e., National Business Lists, Dun & Bradstreet, and Economic Information Systems). Using the March 1976 Bureau of Labor Statistics report on employment and earnings as a standard, the EEO-1 list underrepresents Agriculture and Construction, but EEO-1 contains at least 30% of BLS in all other industries.

COMPARISON OF EEO-1 AND BLS EMPLOYMENT, 1975

	BLS Employment (thousands)	EEO-1 as Percentage of BLS
Agriculture	NA	
Mining	745	58
Construction	3,457	15
Manufacturing	18,347	77
Transportation	4,498	74
Trade	16,947	30
Finance	4,223	51
Service	13,995	30

An advantage of using the EEO-1 list was its manageable size when compared to the other lists. The National Business Lists' 8.7 million records and Dun & Bradstreet's 4.7 million makes extracting data from these lists more costly than from EEO-1's 180,000 records.

Potential EEO-1 respondents are accustomed to being surveyed by EEOC on an annual basis, and were therefore more likely to respond. They are more familiar with employment data retrieval within their organization compared to a company that is not frequently surveyed. Hence, a greater response rate was anticipated.

Names, addresses, and phone numbers from the EEO-1 data file point directly to the person familiar with employment data retrieval, whereas other lists (National Business Lists, Dun & Bradstreet, and Economic Information Systems) identify chief executive officers and other company officials who are not intimately familiar with personnel files.

Appendix B:
Sampling Plan

Overview of Sample Selection Procedures

The sampling objective was to collect 5,000 completed question-
naires representing all sizes and types of business establishments. A
stratified random sampling procedure was used to create two strata of
establishments, one with 100 or more employees and the other with
less than 100. Industries were clustered into four groups using the
Standard Industrial Classification (SIC) code. This use of stratification
was intended to make the sample more efficient by establishing eight
strata that were internally homogeneous regarding industry and size
groupings. These strata were sampled in proportion to their sizes to
insure the required range of industry types and sizes in the sample.

Stratification Design

The two criteria chosen for stratification were size of establishment
in terms of number of persons employed and the Standard Industrial
Classification of the establishment. Size of business was divided into:
(1) 50-99 and (2) 100 or more employees. The 1977 County Business
Patterns (CBP) reveals the following distribution of establishment
sizes:

Establishment Size	Total Employed (Million)
1-4 persons	4.8
5-9	5.7
10-19	7.0
20-49	10.2
50-99	7.6
100-249	8.9

250-499	6.1
500-999	5.2
1000 or more	9.4
TOTAL	64.9 million

A lower limit of 50 employees was set to help protect the confidentiality of employees in responding companies. The 50-employee lower limit also insured that each establishment sampled had the opportunity to have hired a sufficient number of young people to need youth policies and practices.

The distribution of total persons employed in companies with 50-99 and 100 or more persons is as follows:

Establishment Size	Total Employed (Million)
50-99 persons	7.6 (20%)
100 or more	29.6 (80%)

Types of industry were grouped into four clusters based on the volume of young people, 16-24 years old, employed in each SIC industry. Unpublished Current Population Survey (CPS) data from 1980 illustrate the distribution of young people across various industries:

Industry	Youth Ages 16-24 (Thousands)	Distribution of Employed Youth
Agriculture	537	3%
Mining	189	1
Construction	1192	6
Manufacturing	3898	20
Transportation	907	5
Trade	6641	34
Finance	1241	6
Service	4907	25
TOTAL	19,512	100%

Industry types were clustered as follows: (1) manufacturing, (2) trade, (3) service, and (4) agriculture, mining, construction, transportation, and finance.

SAMPLE SIZES BY INDUSTRY CLUSTER AND COMPANY SIZE

Industry Cluster	Distribution of Employed Youth(%)	Number in Cluster	Number Sampled for Each Size	
			50-99(20%)	100 plus (80%)
Manufacturing	20	1000	250	750
Trade	34	1700	425	1275
Service	25	1250	313	938
Agriculture, Mining, Construction, Transportation & Finance	21	1050	262	787
	100	5000	1250	3750

With the 5,000 sample size, the chance was 95 in 100 that results did not vary more than ±3 percentage points from the population values.

The eight strata resulting from two sizes and four industry clusters were sampled in constant proportion.

Appendix C:
The Questionnaire

A SURVEY OF EMPLOYER ATTITUDES
AND
PRACTICES TOWARD HIRING OF YOUTH

October 1981

Dear Sir/Madam:

This questionnaire is part of a nationwide survey about industry's
attitudes and practices toward hiring youth. The goal of the survey is to describe factors that facilitate or impede corporate hiring
of young people 16-24 years old. Your cooperation, therefore, will
be of vital assistance in proposing solutions and recommendations for
greater employment of young people.

This questionnaire will be easy to fill out because, in most instances,
we ask only for approximate answers to be indicated by checking the
appropriate answer space.

Please note that answers to the questionnaire should reflect the perspective of a single plant/establishment or a branch of a business with
several locations. Thus, if your business has multiple branches, the
questionnaire should be filled out by an individual who has a familiarity
with employment information at the particular site where the questionnaire
is received.

Some of the questions ask separately about teenagers aged 16 to 19 and
young adults aged 20 to 24. Where a question doesn't apply to your plant,
establishment or branch, there is a box at the bottom of the age group
to check.

Your participation in this survey is entirely voluntary, and all information
you provide will be treated confidentially.

When you have completed this questionnaire, please return it, if possible
within one week of receipt, in the stamped, addressed envelope enclosed.

A summary of the survey findings will be available to you if you so indicate
on page 10.

Thank you very much for your coopration in this most important survey.

Please note that <u>answers</u> to the questionnaire should reflect the <u>per-</u>
<u>spective of a single plant/establishment of a branch of a business</u>
<u>with several locations</u>. Thus, if your business has multiple branches.
the questionnaire should be filled out by an individual who is familiar
with employment information at the particular stie where the questionnaire is received.

Some of the questions ask separately about teenagers, 16-19, and young
adults, 20-24. Where a question doesn't apply to your plant, establishment, or branch, there is an appropriate box to check.

---

1. Is (your branch of) this Company located in:

    a. Central city or town   ( )
    b. Suburbs   ( )
    c. Rural Area   ( )
    d. Exurbs (between a suburban region and a rural   ( )
        area).

2. What is the primary business activity in your establishment?

    a. Agriculture   ( )
    b. Construction   ( )
    c. Finance   ( )
    d. Manufacturing   ( )
    e. Mining   ( )
    f. Service   ( )
    g. Trade   ( )
    h. Transportation   ( )

3. Do you expect the number of unskilled, semi-skilled, and skilled
    <u>entry-level jobs</u> in your firm to increase, decrease, or remain
    the same over the next five years?

	Probably Increase	Probably Decrease	Probably Remain The Same	Not Applicable
a. Unskilled entry-level jobs	( )	( )	( )	( )
b. Semi-skilled entry-level jobs	( )	( )	( )	( )
c. Skilled entry-level jobs	( )	( )	( )	( )

4. How many employees are in (your branch of) this Company?

    a. Less than 50   ( )
    b. 50-99   ( )
    c. 100 and more   ( )

5. Approximately what percentage of employees in (your branch of) this Company are in the following age categories?

    a. 16 - 19 years old   _____ %
    b. 20 - 24 years old   _____ %
    c. 25 and over   _____ %
        Total Employees   100%

6. Which of the following statements, if any, are true of your Company regarding the hiring of different age groups of youth? (CHECK AS MANY AS APPLY IN EACH COLUMN.)

	Teenagers 16-19	Adults 20-24
a. Hire for unskilled jobs	( )	( )
b. Hire for part-time jobs	( )	( )
c. Hire for entry-level jobs	( )	( )
d. Hire those with experience	( )	( )
e. Hire for any job not prohibited by child labor laws	( )	( )
f. WE DO NOT HIRE PEOPLE IN THIS AGE GROUP AT ALL	( )	( )

7. Which <u>one</u> of the following factors contributes <u>most</u> to the turnover rate among <u>full-time</u> young employees in your Company? (CHECK ONE FOR EACH AGE CATEGORY.)

	Teeangers 16-19	Adults 20-24
a. Quitting or resigning	( )	( )
b. Firing or dismissal	( )	( )
c. Returning to school	( )	( )
d. Leaving for better job	( )	( )
e. Family moving or relocating	( )	( )
f. Being laid off by the Company	( )	( )
g. Summer or temporary employment	( )	( )
h. Other factors (PLEASE SPECIFY)	( )	( )

_____

    i. WE DO NOT HIRE PEOPLE IN THIS AGE GROUP AT ALL   ( )   ( )

8. Compared to employees who are 25 years of age and over, how would
    you generally characterize the younger people employed by your
    firm?

	Teenagers 16-19	Adults 20-24

Younger employees compared to
employees 25 years of age or older

a. Punctuality:

	Teenagers 16-19	Adults 20-24
Better	( )	( )
The Same	( )	( )
Poorer	( )	( )

b. Retention:

Better	( )	( )
The Same	( )	( )
Poorer	( )	( )

c. Absences:

Fewer	( )	( )
The Same	( )	( )
More	( )	( )

d. Productivity:

Better	( )	( )
The Same	( )	( )
Poorer	( )	( )

e. Discipline:

Better	( )	( )
The Same	( )	( )
Poorer	( )	( )

f. Training Costs:

Lower	( )	( )
The Same	( )	( )
Higher	( )	( )

g. Time and Costs of Supervision:

Lower	( )	( )
The Same	( )	( )
Higher	( )	( )

9. At what <u>one</u> position are employees in the following age groups <u>most</u> concentrated in your Company? (CHECK ONE FOR EACH AGE CATEGORY.)

		Teenagers 16-19	Adults 20-24
a.	Professional/Technical/Managerial	( )	( )
b.	Craftsman	( )	( )
c.	Sales	( )	( )
d.	Clerical	( )	( )
e.	Operatives	( )	( )
f.	Services	( )	( )
g.	Laborers	( )	( )
h.	WE DO NOT HIRE PEOPLE IN THIS AGE GROUP AT ALL	( )	( )

10. What kinds of training programs are available for <u>new</u> young employees in the positions where they are <u>most</u> concentrated? (CHECK ALL THAT APPLY IN EACH COLUMN.)

		Teenagers 16-19	Adults 20-24
a.	On-the-job training (OJT)	( )	( )
b.	Apprenticeship training	( )	( )
c.	In-service	( )	( )
d.	Other (PLEASE SPECIFY)	( )	( )
e.	None	( )	( )
f.	WE DO NOT HIRE PEOPLE IN THIS AGE GROUP AT ALL	( )	(.)

11. To what extent are opportunities for advancement in your Company provided in the positions where young employees are <u>most</u> concentrated? (PLACE ONLY ONE CHECK IN EACH COLUMN.)

		Teenagers 16-19	Adults 20-24
a.	A great extent	( )	( )
b.	Some	( )	( )
c.	Very little	( )	( )
d.	None	( )	( )
e.	WE DO NOT HIRE PEOPLE IN THIS AGE GROUP AT ALL	( )	( )

12. What effect do you think a sub-minimum wage differential for youth
     will have on industry's hiring of youth?

    a. Will increase the number of jobs available to youth   ( )

    b. Will decrease the number of jobs available to youth   ( )

    c. Will have no effect on the number of jobs available   ( )
     to youth

    d. Other (PLEASE SPECIFY):   ( )

             _____

13. In your judgement, how important are the following in-school efforts
     toward making youth more employable? (PLACE ONE CHECK IN EACH ROW.)

		Very Important	Somewhat Important	Not Important
a.	Concentrating efforts on teaching basic reading, writing, and math skills	( )	( )	( )
b.	Providing more students with practical world-of-work orientation	( )	( )	( )
c.	Involving industry in curriculum development	( )	( )	( )
d.	Other (PLEASE SPECIFY):	( )	( )	( )

             _____

             _____

14. How important do you think are the following efforts by private industry
     in improving the employability of youth? (PLACE ONE CHECK IN EACH ROW.)

		Very Important	Somewhat Important	Not Important
a.	Providing short-term work experience for students to become aware of industry's needs	( )	( )	( )
b.	Providing more skill training on the job	( )	( )	( )
c.	Creating stronger linkages with job development and placement agencies	( )	( )	( )
d.	Aiding educators in developing job-related curricula	( )	( )	( )
e.	Creating non-traditional apprenticeship programs (e.g., computer programming)	( )	( )	( )
f.	Other (PLEASE SPECIFY):	( )	( )	( )

             _____

15. Please indicate if you have heard of the following government incentives for hiring youth, whether your Company has used any in the last 12 months, and the reasons it has or has not.

	Incentive	Heard of Yes	Heard of No	Used Yes	Used No	Reason(s) used or not used (Use appropriate codes from below.)(USE AS MANY AS APPLY.)
a.	Targeted Jobs Tax Credit 1978	( )	( )	( )	( )	
b.	Work Incentive Program (WIN)	( )	( )	( )	( )	
c.	Job Corps	( )	( )	( )	( )	
d.	CETA On-the-Job Training (OJT) Subsidies	( )	( )	( )	( )	
e.	SPEDY Summer Youth Program	( )	( )	( )	( )	
f.	CETA Job Upgrading and Retraining Programs	( )	( )	( )	( )	
g.	CETA Youth Employment and Training Programs (YETP)	( )	( )	( )	( )	
h.	Industry Work Experience Programs (IWEP)	( )	( )	( )	( )	
i.	Sub-Minimum Wage Certificates for Youth	( )	( )	( )	( )	
j.	Work Equity Program (WEP)	( )	( )	( )	( )	

Codes for Reasons Used

1. Benefit to our firm because of of subsidy
2. Good source of labor
3. Help reduce unemployment
4. No particular reason
5. Other (PLEASE SPECIFY):

_____

Codes for Reasons NOT Used

a. Unaware of program
b. Too much red tape
c. Lacked enough information to become involved
d. Program does not seem as if it will benefit our firm
e. Have never been approached by any of the agencies
f. Other (PLEASE SPECIFY):

_____

16. In the last 12 months, did your Company hire many more, about the same, or fewer <u>minority</u> youths aged 16-24 than in the previous year? (PLACE ONLY ONE CHECK IN EACH ROW.)

Minority Hired	Many More	About the Same	Fewer	None at All
a. American Indian or Alaskan Native	( )	( )	( )	( )
b. Asian or Pacific Islander	( )	( )	( )	( )
c. Black, not of Hispanic Origin	( )	( )	( )	( )
d. Hispanic	( )	( )	( )	( )
e. Other racial minorities (SPECIFY)				
_____	( )	( )	( )	( )
_____	( )	( )	( )	( )

17. In which <u>one</u> position do minority youth employed by your Company tend to be <u>most</u> concentrated? (CHECK ONLY ONE.)

   a. Professional/Technical/Managerial   ( )
   b. Craftsman   ( )
   c. Sales   ( )
   d. Clerical   ( )
   e. Operatives   ( )
   f. Service   ( )
   g. Laborer   ( )

18. What would you (your Company) recommend as an effective means to hire more minority youth?

   _____
   _____
   _____
   _____

19. Would your Company be willing to hire more minority youth if offered a wage subsidy of:

	Yes	No
a. 50%	( )	( )
b. 75%	( )	( )
c. 100%	( )	( )

20. Does your Company currently have a special jobs program for <u>minority</u> youth?

   a. Yes   ( )

   b. No, had one previously   ( ) ┐
   C. No, never had one   ( ) ┘── STOP PLEASE. DO NOT COMPLETE THE REST OF THIS QUESTIONNAIRE. THANK YOU FOR YOUR COOPERATION.

21. Approximately how many minority youths aged 16-24 participated in your jobs program during its latest complete year of operation?

    _____

22. Who funds the minority youth jobs program in your Company?   (CHECK ALL THAT APPLY.)

    a. Funded by your Company   ( )
    b. Funded by the Federal Government   ( )
    c. Funded by State/Local Government   ( )
    d. Funded by unions   ( )
    e. Funded by other (SPECIFY) _____   ( )
    f. Don't know.   ( )

23. How successful do you consider your Company's jobs program for minority youth in terms of achieving its goals?

    a. Successful   ( )
    b. Somewhat successful   ( )
    c. Unsuccessful   ( )
    d. Somewhat unsuccessful   ( )
    e. Don't know   ( )

24. What do you expect will be your Company's level of participation in its jobs program for minority youth over the next two years?

    a. Participation will remain about the same   ( )
    b. Participation will increase   ( )
    c. Participation will decrease   ( )
    d. Don't know   ( )

25. Over the past year, which one of the following factors accounted for the most turnovers among full-time minority youth employees who participated in your Company's job program?   (PLACE ONE CHECK IN EACH COLUMN.)

		Teenagers 16-19	Adults 20-24
a.	Quitting or resigning	( )	( )
b.	Firing or dismissal	( )	( )
c.	Returning to school	( )	( )
d.	Leaving for better job	( )	( )
e.	Family moving or relocating	( )	( )
f.	Being laid off by the Company	( )	( )
g.	Summer or temporary employment	( )	( )
g.	Other (PLEASE SPECIFY):	( )	( )

    _____

    | i. | WE DO NOT HIRE PEOPLE FROM THIS AGE GROUP AT ALL | ( ) | ( ) |

26. Please feel free to add other comments about your Company's job
     program.

     _____

     _____

     _____

     _____

     _____

     _____

                   THANK YOU FOR YOUR COOPERATION!

     PLEASE FORWARD A SUMMARY OF SURVEY FINDINGS.   YES ( )   NO ( )

Appendix D:
Supporting Tables

TABLE A
HIRING PATTERNS FOR BLACK YOUTHS COMPARED TO PREVIOUS
YEAR, BY TYPE OF BUSINESS
(PERCENTAGE DISTRIBUTION)

Pattern	Business				
	Manufacturing	Trade	Finance	Service	Other[a/]
Hired Many More	7	17	14	15	17
Hired About the Same	56	69	71	71	43
Hired Fewer/ None	37	14	16	14	40
Total	100	100	100	100	100
Sample Size	(84)	(129)	(44)	(140)	(35)

a. Other businesses include mining, agriculture, construction, and transportation.
Note: Percentages may not add to 100 due to rounding.

TABLE B
HIRING PATTERNS OF BLACK YOUTHS COMPARED TO PREVIOUS
YEAR, BY SIZE OF BUSINESS
(PERCENTAGE DISTRIBUTION)

	Size		
Pattern	Small (1-99)	Medium (100-249)	Large) (250 & over)
Hired Many More	15	15	12
Hired About the Same	61	64	69
Hired Fewer/ None	24	20	19
Total	100	100	100
Sample Size	(80)	(213)	(139)

Note: Percentages may not add to 100 due to rounding.

TABLE C
HIRING PATTERNS OF BLACK YOUTHS COMPARED TO PREVIOUS
YEAR, BY LOCATION OF BUSINESS
(PERCENTAGE DISTRIBUTION)

	Location		
Pattern	Central City/Town	Suburbs	Exurbs/Rural
Hired Many More	16	15	9
Hired About the Same	66	70	52
Hired Fewer/ None	19	15	39
Total	100	100	100
Sample Size	(256)	(146)	(82)

Note: Percentages may not add to 100 due to rounding.

TABLE D
HIRING PATTERNS OF BLACK YOUTHS COMPARED TO PREVIOUS
YEAR, BY REGION
(PERCENTAGE DISTRIBUTION)

	Region			
Pattern	Northeast	North Central	West	South
Hired Many More	11	11	21	16
Hired About the Same	57	61	56	79
Hired Fewer/ None	33	28	23	5
Total	100	100	100	100
Sample Size	(83)	(142)	(80)	(135)

Note: Percentages may not add to 100 due to rounding.

TABLE E
HIRING PATTERNS OF HISPANIC YOUTHS COMPARED TO PREVIOUS
YEAR, BY TYPE OF BUSINESS
(PERCENTAGE DISTRIBUTION)

	Business				
Pattern	Manufacturing	Trade	Finance	Service	Other[a]
Hired Many More	12	14	18	12	17
Hired About the Same	35	58	56	59	40
Hired Fewer/ None	51	28	26	30	42
Total	100	100	100	100	100
Sample Size	(82)	(120)	(39)	(128)	(35)

a. Other businesses include mining, agriculture, construction, and transportation.
Note: Percentages may not add to 100 due to rounding.

TABLE F
HIRING PATTERNS OF HISPANIC YOUTHS COMPARED TO PREVIOUS
YEAR, BY SIZE OF BUSINESS
(PERCENTAGE DISTRIBUTION)

Pattern	Size		
	Small (1-99)	Medium (100-249)	Large (250 & over)
Hired Many More	15	13	14
Hired About the Same	56	49	55
Hired Fewer/ None	29	38	32
Total	100	100	100
Sample Size	(75)	(196)	(133)

Note: Percentages may not add to 100 due to rounding.

TABLE G
HIRING PATTERNS OF HISPANIC YOUTHS COMPARED TO PREVIOUS
YEAR, BY LOCATION OF BUSINESS
(PERCENTAGE DISTRIBUTION)

Pattern	Location		
	Central City/Town	Suburbs	Exurbs/Rural
Hired Many More	14	12	13
Hired About the Same	54	53	34
Hired Fewer/ None	32	35	53
Total	100	100	100
Sample Size	(232)	(137)	(79)

Note: Percentages may not add to 100 due to rounding.

TABLE H
HIRING PATTERNS OF HISPANIC YOUTHS COMPARED TO PREVIOUS
YEAR, BY REGION
(PERCENTAGE DISTRIBUTION)

	Region			
Pattern	Northeast	North Central	West	South
Hired Many More	11	9	28	11
Hired About the Same	47	45	62	55
Hired Fewer/ None	42	46	10	33
Total	100	100	100	100
Sample Size	(79)	(130)	(78)	(123)

Note: Percentages may not add to 100 due to rounding.

TABLE I
EXPECTATIONS FOR GROWTH OF UNSKILLED JOBS OVER THE NEXT
FIVE YEARS, BY SIZE OF BUSINESS
(PERCENTAGE DISTRIBUTION)

	Size		
Expectations	Small (1-99)	Medium (100-249)	Large (250 & over)
Probably Increase	29	26	21
Probably Decrease	17	18	14
Probably Remain the Same	54	56	65
Total	100	100	100
Sample Size	(70)	(199)	(136)

Note: Percentages may not add to 100 due to rounding.

TABLE J
EXPECTATIONS FOR GROWTH OF UNSKILLED JOBS OVER THE NEXT
FIVE YEARS, BY LOCATION OF BUSINESS
(PERCENTAGE DISTRIBUTION)

Expectations	Location		
	Central City/Town	Suburbs	Rural/Exurbs
Probably Increase	22	25	27
Probably Decrease	18	16	13
Probably Remain the Same	60	59	60
Total	100	100	100
Sample Size	(232)	(141)	(84)

Note: Percentages may not add to 100 due to rounding.

TABLE K
EXPECTATIONS FOR GROWTH OF UNSKILLED JOBS OVER THE NEXT
FIVE YEARS, BY REGION
(PERCENTAGE DISTRIBUTION)

Expectations	Region			
	Northeast	North Central	West	South
Probably Increase	22	20	30	30
Probably Decrease	17	19	17	12
Probably Remain the Same	62	62	53	58
Total	100	100	100	100
Sample Size	(79)	(135)	(77)	(122)

Note: Percentages may not add to 100 due to rounding.

TABLE L
EXPECTATIONS FOR GROWTH OF SEMISKILLED JOBS OVER THE
NEXT FIVE YEARS, BY SIZE OF BUSINESS
(PERCENTAGE DISTRIBUTION)

	Size		
Expectations	Small (1-99)	Medium (100-249)	Large (250 & over)
Probably Increase	37	37	32
Probably Decrease	5	8	8
Probably Remain the Same	58	55	60
Total	100	100	100
Sample Size	(76)	(211)	(143)

Note: Percentages may not add to 100 due to rounding.

TABLE M
EXPECTATIONS FOR GROWTH OF SEMISKILLED JOBS OVER THE
NEXT FIVE YEARS, BY LOCATION OF BUSINESS
(PERCENTAGE DISTRIBUTION)

	Location		
Expectations	Central City/Town	Suburbs	Rural/Exurbs
Probably Increase	37	26	41
Probably Decrease	8	10	8
Probably Remain the Same	55	65	51
Total	100	100	100
Sample Size	(255)	(145)	(85)

Note: Percentages may not add to 100 due to rounding.

TABLE N
EXPECTATIONS FOR GROWTH OF SEMISKILLED JOBS OVER THE
NEXT FIVE YEARS, BY REGION
(PERCENTAGE DISTRIBUTION)

	Region			
Expectations	Northeast	North Central	West	South
Probably Increase	33	30	42	38
Probably Decrease	8	11	7	5
Probably Remain the Same	60	59	51	58
Total	100	100	100	100
Sample Size	(80)	(144)	(82)	(132)

Note: Percentages may not add to 100 due to rounding.

TABLE O
EXPECTATIONS FOR GROWTH OF SKILLED JOBS OVER THE NEXT
FIVE YEARS, BY SIZE OF BUSINESS
(PERCENTAGE DISTRIBUTION)

	Size		
Expectations	Small (1-99)	Medium (100-249)	Large (250 & over)
Probably Increase	39	45	44
Probably Decrease	6	5	6
Probably Remain the Same	55	50	50
Total	100	100	100
Sample Size	(78)	(206)	(142)

Note: Percentages may not add to 100 due to rounding.

TABLE P
EXPECTATIONS FOR GROWTH OF SKILLED JOBS OVER THE NEXT
FIVE YEARS, BY LOCATION OF BUSINESS
(PERCENTAGE DISTRIBUTION)

	Location		
Expectations	Central City/Town	Suburbs	Rural/Exurbs
Probably Increase	44	34	52
Probably Decrease	6	8	6
Probably Remain the Same	50	58	42
Total	100	100	100
Sample Size	(248)	(144)	(83)

Note: Percentages may not add to 100 due to rounding.

TABLE Q
EXPECTATIONS FOR GROWTH OF SKILLED JOBS OVER THE NEXT
FIVE YEARS, BY REGION
(PERCENTAGE DISTRIBUTION)

	Region			
Expectations	Northeast	North Central	West	South
Probably Increase	43	40	51	43
Probably Decrease	4	7	8	5
Probably Remain the Same	54	54	41	52
Total	100	100	100	100
Sample Size	(82)	(137)	(83)	(130)

Note: Percentages may not add to 100 due to rounding.

Bibliography

Barton, Paul E.
    1975   "Youth Employment and Career Entry." In *Labor Market Information for Youth*. Seymour L. Wolfbein, ed. Philadelphia: Temple University Press.

Bullock, Paul
    1972   *Youth in the Labor Market: Employment Patterns and Career Aspirations in Watts and East Los Angeles*. Washington, D.C.: U.S. Department of Labor Manpower Administration (January).

Butler, Erik Payne, and Darr, James
    1980   *Research on Youth Employment and Employability Development: Educator and Employer Perspectives*. Waltham, Mass.: Brandeis University Press (May).

Chamber of Commerce of the United States
    1978   *A Survey of Federal Employment and Training Programs*. Washington, D.C.: Chamber of Commerce of the United States (September).

Cohen, Eli, et al.
    1965   *Getting Hired, Getting Trained: A Study of Industry Practices and Policies on Youth Employment*. Washington, D.C.: U.S. Government Printing Office.

Cook, Fred S., and Lanham, Frank
    1966   *Opportunities and Requirements for Initial Employment of School Learners with Emphasis on Office and Retail Jobs*. Detroit: Wayne State University Press.

Diamond, Daniel E., and Bedrosian, Hrach
    1970   *Industry Hiring Requirements and Employment of Disadvantaged Groups*. New York: New York University School of Commerce.

Freedman, Marcia
    1976   "The Youth Labor Market." In *From School to Work: Improving the Transition*. Washington, D.C.: National Commission for Manpower Policy.

Freeman, Richard B.
    1980   "Why Is There a Youth Labor Market Problem?" In *Youth Employment and Public Policy*. Bernard E. Anderson and Isabel Sawhill, eds. Englewood Cliffs, N.J.: Prentice-Hall.

Greenleigh Associates, Inc.
    1970   *The Job Opportunities in the Business Sector Program: An Evaluation of Impact of Ten Standard Metropolitan Statistical Area* New York: Greenleigh Associates.

Hill, Robert B.
    1978   *The Illusion of Black Progress*. Washington, D.C.: National Urban League Research Department.

————.

1980   "Discrimination and Minority Youth Unemployment." In *A Review of Youth Employment, Programs, Policies*. Washington, D.C.: The Vice-President's Task Force on Youth Employment.

Janger, Allen R.

1972   *Employing the Disadvantaged: A Company Perspective*. New York: The Conference Board.

Lusterman, Seymour, and Gorlin, Harriet

1980   *Educating Students for Work: Some Business Roles*. New York: The Conference Board.

Lynton, Edith, et al.

1978   *Employers' Views on Hiring and Training*. New York: Labor Market Information.

McGhee, James D.

1982   "The Black Teenager: An Endangered Species." In *State of Black America, 1982*. New York: National Urban League.

National Child Labor Committee

1976   *Rites of Passage: The Crisis of Youth's Transition from School to Work*. New York: National Child Labor Committee.

National Commission for Manpower Policy

1976   "Corporate Hiring Practices." In *From School to Work: Improving the Transition*. Washington, D.C.: National Commission for Manpower Policy.

————.

1978   *An Enlarged Role for the Private Sector in Federal Employment and Training Programs*. Report no. 8. Washington, D.C.: National Commission for Manpower Policy.

————.

1978   *Increasing Job Opportunities in the Private Sector*. Special Report no. 29. Washington, D.C.: National Commission for Manpower Policy.

National Manpower Institute

1973   *A Study of Corporate Youth Employment Policies and Practices*. Washington, D.C.: National Manpower Institute.

Osterman, Paul

1979   "The Employment Problems of Black Youth: A Review of the Evidence and Some Policy Suggestions." In *Expanding Employment Opportunities for Disadvantaged Youth: Sponsored Research*. Washington, D.C.: National Commission for Employment Policy.

Parnes, Herbert S., and Kohen, Andrew I.

1971   *Career Thresholds: A Longitudinal Study of the Educational and Labor Market Experience of Male Youth*. Center for Human Resources Research. Columbus, Oh.: Ohio State University Press (June).

Robison, David

1979   *Small Business Employment and the Work Preparation of Youth*. Washington, D.C.: Vice-President's Task Force on Youth Employment.

Schewegler, Paul W.
  1979   *Human Resources: A Profile and Design for the 80s.* Redondo Beach, Calif.: TRW Defense and Space Systems Group.
Solow, Robert M.
  1980   "Employment Policy in Inflationery Times." In *Employing the Unemployed.* Eli Ginzberg, ed. New York: Basic Books.
Taggart, Robert
  1981   *A Fisherman's Guide: An Assessment of Training and Remediation Strategies.* Kalamazoo, Mich.: W. E. Upjohn Institute for Employment Research.
The White House
  1980   *A Summary Report of the Vice-President's Task Force on Youth Employment.* Washington, D.C.: The White House.
Toeffler, Alvin
  1983   "A Look at the Future." National Urban League Annual Conference. New Orleans: Louisiana.
U.S. Department of Labor
  1971   *Involving Private Employers in CETA Programs: A Case Study.* R & D Monograph 75. Washington, D.C.: U.S. Department of Labor Employment and Training Administration.

  _____.
  1978   *Conference Report on Youth Unemployment: Its Measurement and Meaning.* Washington, D.C.: U.S. Department of Labor Employment and Training Administration.

  _____.
  1980   *The Nature of the Youth Employment Problem: A Review Paper.* Technical Analysis Paper. Washington, D.C.: U.S. Department of Labor (March).
Vaughn-Cooke, Denys
  1980   "Causes of Teenage and Youth Unemployment." Unpublished paper. Washington, D.C.: Urban Institute (June).
Williams, Walter E.
  1977   "Youth and Minority Unemployment: U.S. Congress Joint Economic Committee. Washington, D.C.: U.S. Government Printing Office (July 6).
Work in America Institute, Inc.
  1979   *Job Strategies for Urban Youth: Sixteen Pilot Programs for Action.* Scarsdale, N.Y.: Work in America Institute.
Youth Programs
  1982   "Do Work Attitudes Matter?" The Center for Employment and Income Studies. Waltham, Mass.: Brandeis University Press (Winter).
Youth Work, Inc.
  1980   *Review of the Literature: Expanded Private Sector Involvement.* Washington, D.C.: Youth Work.